"Jim Garlow's work is so timely! At this revival juncture in the Church, sensitive and sensible leaders are seeking ways to establish and equip the whole body of the congregation. Just as prayer and an openness to the Holy Spirit are the keys to the Church's awakening, the concepts in *Partners in Ministry* are the keys to the Church's activation for ministry."

Jack W. Hayford, Senior Pastor
The Church on the Way
Van Nuys, California

"This is one of the most readable and most helpful manuals for church members I have ever seen. In *Partners in Ministry*, Dr. Garlow has managed to communicate in a way that is soundly theological yet as clear and easy to understand as a child's primer. Whether his subject has to do with the Church's biblical foundation or its history or its ministerial functions, he has injected a contagious enthusiasm and sense of inspiration into every page. Clever illustrations serve to keep readers' interest at a high level throughout. From training to serving to sharing gifts, the emphasis of the direct kind of leadership training that will equip them to become exemplary colaborers with Christ in His Church. Heartily recommended."

Dr. D. James Kennedy, Senior Minister
Coral Ridge Presbyterian Church
Fort Lauderdale, Florida

"This book is the answer to the need of everyone who attends church. Teaching requires knowledge, while learning calls for desire. The twin occupations of intellectual life are teaching and learning for those who desire to grow and mature. Jim's teachings are fundamental and mandatory."

Edwin Louis Cole, Founder and President
Christian Men's Network
Grapevine, Texas

"To be a purpose-driven church, you must mobilize every member for ministry. Jim Garlow's prac'·
ber for ministry. Jim Garlow's prac'·
toward that goal. It contains bibli(
audience into an army!"

Dr. Rick Warren, Senior P
Saddleback Valley Comm
Lake Forest, California

"The Reformation gave voice to the priesthood of all believers, but John Wesley's genius for mobilizing and equipping laity for ministry made the doctrine come alive. Forces of renewal were set in motion in the ensuing awakening that still have reverberations around the world. No one tells the story better than Jim Garlow."

Dr. Robert E. Coleman, Professor and Director
Billy Graham School of World Mission and Evangelism
Trinity International University
Deerfield, Illinois

"The hope for an effective, aggressive, and enabled church in our world today is for laypeople to take back the work of the church and allow their shepherds to go about the business of casting vision and equipping them. It will only be as pastors and laypeople become passionate about the commission of Christ and join their hearts and hands to fulfill His assignment that nations will pause long enough to see if we are real and sincere. *Partners in Ministry* will assist us as we take the first steps toward that goal."

H. B. London Jr.
Vice President, Ministry Outreach/
Pastoral Ministries
Focus on the Family

"In my opinion, the most effective churches of the future will be those that practice giving ministry to the laity. In his book *Partners in Ministry* Jim Garlow outlines biblically and practically how this can happen in a local church. It is an excellent resource to help churches teach and practice that every member is a minister."

John Ed Mathison, Senior Pastor
Frazer Memorial United Methodist Church
Montgomery, Alabama

"It is my privilege to teach lay ministry to thousands of people each year. Jim Garlow's book *Partners in Ministry* has influenced me more than any other book on this vital subject. It is a 'must read' for any person who desires to have an effective ministry for God."

John C. Maxwell
Author, Speaker, and Founder of Injoy, Inc.

"Just about every pastor agrees that the day of clericalism is over. Yet hundreds of pastors still find themselves doing just about all the ministry of the church, mainly because they don't know how to make the necessary changes. Jim Garlow does, and I know no better book than *Partners in Ministry* for helping lay people move into the dins of ministry that will be incredibly fulfilling for them as individuals and bring new health and vitality to the church."

Dr. C. Peter Wagner, Professor
Fuller Theological Seminary
Pasadena, California
Director
International Prayer Center
Colorado Springs, Colorado

"If every church would get hold of the simple truth in Jim Garlow's book *Partners in Ministry*—that every Christian is a minister and not just a layperson—I believe the church in America would be revolutionized. Jim's book is practical, with many illustrations and graphs to prove his points. He also includes information about John Wesley's training of the laity based on the four themes of being called, gifted, trained, and sent into ministry."

Stephen Strang, President and CEO
Strang Communications Company
Lake Mary, Florida

"*Partners in Ministry* is an enjoyable read for all Christians. Dr. Jim Garlow has presented us with a book that ministers and laypeople should read. Rich in the history and philosophy of John Wesley, this book is a pleasure to read—and an inspiration. We are indeed 'partners in ministry,' sharing the same responsibility. This book helps us to work together."

Thomas H. Ken, President
Drew University
Madison, New Jersey
Former Governor of New Jersey
State Capitol
Trenton, New Jersey

"Dr. James Garlow has not only an understanding and heart for lay ministry . . . he has a passion for it. He teaches it . . . and preaches it . . . and exemplifies it in his own life. In the 30 years that I have known him, he has never wavered from that cause. The design of God could not be clearer . . . as believers sharing together in this redemptive society called the Church, we are all involved in mutual ministry. This book, *Partners in Ministry*, lays out perfectly the definitive plan of how laity and clergy merge their gifts and opportunities for the glory of the Father. This book is more than a remarkable study guide and profound treatise . . . it lifts your heart with his . . . and His. Other writings can tell you what to do. This one goes one step beyond that . . . it tells you how to feel."

Derric Johnson, Artist in Residence
George Fox University
Newburg, Oregon
Music Consultant and Show Director
Walt Disney World
Orlando, Florida

"The number one issue of the Church is lay ministry. Jim Garlow has given us a very clear blueprint as to how that ministry can be equipped and unleashed. This book is a 'must read' for pastors and laity."

Dr. Maxie D. Dunnam, President
Asbury Theological Seminary
Wilmore, Kentucky

"Nothing takes precedence over training and mobilizing the laity . . . Jim Garlow has said it well in *Partners in Ministry*. It's a must!"

Bob Moorehead, Senior Pastor
Overlake Christian Church
Kirkland, Washington

"In this well-researched, biblical treatise, the author closes the gap separating laypeople and pastors and does so in a very convincing manner."

Dr. Jon Johnston, Professor of Sociology
Pepperdine University
Malibu, California

"When and where ministry is shared together, the church thrives, and when the ministry is carried on wholly by the elite professional clergy, the church dies. All cutting-edge churches in our world today have rediscovered the truth of Dr. Garlow's masterful book, *Partners in Ministry*. And, along with the author, have found practical ways to help all Christians discover their special gifts and begin using them in the ministry. No book could be more needed or more timely for pastors and laity to read together than this special gift that my friend Jim Garlow gives to the Church."

Dr. Dale E. Galloway, Dean
Beeson International Center for Biblical Preaching and
Church Leadership
Asbury Theological Seminary
Wilmore, Kentucky
Founding Pastor
New Hope Community Church
Portland, Oregon

"The only way a church can ever reach its spiritual and natural potential is by the pastor, staff, and congregation working together. Even Jesus needed His disciples. Dr. Jim Garlow's book *Partners in Ministry* will help your church reach the vision God has given you in His Word and in your heart."

Bob Yandian, Senior Pastor
Grace Fellowship
Tulsa, Oklahoma

"Today we are seeing a renewed emphasis on the ministry as the work of all God's people, a common calling growing out of our baptism. Jim Garlow's work provides a solid foundation for the rediscovery of what was essential to the Church in the New Testament and characteristic of John Wesley's Methodist movement. It calls for a strong partnership between clergy and laity in this shared task and invites the whole Church to reclaim the call to serve Christ in all of life."

John E. Harnish, Associate General Secretary of the
Section of Elders and Local Pastors
General Board of Higher Education and Ministry
The United Methodist Church
Nashville, Tennessee

"Can one book really change a person's life? The answer is yes! I am a layman, and for the last 25 years I have been training laity in ministry. *Partners in Ministry* is the best book out there to help a person understand lay ministry and teach it to others."

Leonard C. Albert, Executive Director
Department of Lay Ministries
Church of God
Cleveland, Tennessee

"Jim Garlow persuasively challenges Christians to move from being passive spectators to active participants in the ministry of their congregations. *Partners in Ministry* thoughtfully and accurately explores the biblical basis and historical precedence for lay ministry. The delightful combination of anecdotes, simple charts, and visual illustrations makes it fascinating to read and its principles easy to remember and apply. This book will be valuable to pastors striving to equip their congregations and to laypeople eager to identify, develop, and use their God-given gifts. While the emphasis is upon lay ministry, it exalts rather than diminishes the role of the pastor. Readers will want to retain this volume to stimulate discussion or to provide helpful guidance in planning and implementing lay ministries."

Dr. Daniel R. Chamberlain, President
Houghton College
Houghton, New York

"Historically Methodism, along with other denominational movements, grew rapidly in America due to the extensive use of laity. *Partners in Ministry* takes the mystery out of equipping the laity for ministry. This manual skillfully gives the leaders the transferable tools that come out of Wesley's passion for people and his desire to equip lifelong ministers. It allows the leader to adjust Wesley's methods to utilize individual gifts and conforms to basic personality traits. This is a clear, precise work, and I am excited about it."

Dr. Gordon Coulter, Professor of Christian Education and
Director of Field Education
Haggard Graduate School of Theology
Azusa Pacific University
Azusa, California

"Jim Garlow has written a very timely and helpful book. The entire Christian community can benefit from this well-written book because all of us have awakened to the realization that the baptism of all Christians is their ordination into ministry. Jim reinforces that truth and shows us in a very practical way how to mobilize and equip our laity for ministry."

Dr. William U. Hinson, Pastor
The First United Methodist Church
Houston, Texas

"Pastor, *Partners in Ministry* is a book you will want to order in quantity for your leaders. In this book, Dr. Garlow has captured the vital concept of partnership that must be restored in today's church. Use it to further equip your leaders, to better help them understand their calling in ministry. Don't just tell them to read it. Assign them a chapter, then discuss it with them. Proper use of this book could revolutionize your church."

Karen Hurston, Director and Founder
Hurston Ministries and Consultation Service
Gulf Breeze, Florida

"I couldn't accomplish all that I have in the ministry without help. No minister can. Laypeople are vital to the success of one's vision. Jim Garlow helps us to understand the importance of lay ministry, and he carefully outlines the steps necessary to help people find their gifts and function in the ministry of the local church. His book has blessed my life, and I know it will bless others. If a pastor is truly going to pastor his people, he needs to read Jim's book."

Buddy Harrison, Founder and President
Faith Christian Fellowship International
Tulsa, Oklahoma
Chairman
Harrison House Publishing
Tulsa, Oklahoma

"When *Partners in Ministry* first appeared, it was a much-needed guide for lay involvement. It is even more timely to reappear in late century. Ministry must involve laypersons at every level. This book can serve as an effective tool for church staff to use in equipping and training lay leaders for the harvest."

Dr. Loren P. Gresham, President
Southern Nazarene University
Bethany, Oklahoma

"For years *Partners in Ministry* has been a book I return to for a biblical understanding of equipping laity for ministry. Since my ministry has always emphasized lay ministry, I have shelves of good books about it. For real meat, I return to Dr. Garlow's *Partners in Ministry*. It is sound biblically. It is proven in practice. I have given away scores of copies to friends. I recommend it highly."

Dr. David L. Brazelton, District Superintendent
Tampa District, United Methodist Church
Tampa, Florida

"Jim Garlow's book *Partners in Ministry* is a must for both pastors and laity. I have personally utilized the material and employed the principles contained in this book for more than a decade in the church I pastor. The application of the principle of laity and pastors working together is an absolute necessity if any local church is to be a growing body of believers. Jim Garlow writes with clarity and passion. His sources are well documented. *Partners in Ministry* is an excellent textbook for motivating and training laity for ministry. From his many years of studying church history, Jim Garlow has written a masterful manuscript on the premier principle for church growth, laity and pastors working together."

J. Don George, Senior Pastor
Calvary Temple
Irving, Texas

"I would expect a book titled *Partners in Ministry* with a subtitle *Laity and Pastors Working Together* to be clear and comprehensible for laypeople, while being instructive and enlightening for clergy. This book is both. Dr. Jim Garlow uses biblical teachings, skilled writing, educative diagrams, and illuminating art to create a level playing field so volunteer and vocational ministers can be authentic partners in ministry. For 10 years I have used many of Jim's tradition-modifying concepts, historical data, and smart diagrams in my seminars. I shall look forward to this effective tool of the Second Reformation."

Dr. Mel Seinbron, Founder and President
Lay Pastors Ministry, Inc.
Minneapolis, Minnesota
Pastoral Staff Member
Hope Presbyterian Church
Ricefield, Minnesota

"The Great Commission of Jesus is addressed to all believers, not to a select few. Every follower of our Lord is called to, and gifted for, ministry. Dr. Jim Garlow powerfully expresses this truth in his book *Partners in Ministry*. Elton Trueblood once stated, "The 16th century church gave the Bible to the laity. Now we must give the ministry to them." Every pastor and layperson who reads and prayerfully studies this biblically sound presentation will be enlightened and challenged to heightened ministry."

Dr. John A. Knight, General Superintendent
Church of the Nazarene International Headquarters
Kansas City

"The training and mobilization of the laity is the central key to both church growth and church renewal. Jim Garlow has written a primer on laity and pastors pastoring together to do the ministry of the church. His paradigm directs pastors to encourage and enable the laity to discover and develop their spiritual gifts and then to deploy them into ministry. This book is essential for a true understanding of contemporary ministry and is recommended for the laity and especially for church leaders and pastors."

Dr. Earl E. Grant, Professor
Haggard Graduate School of Theology
Azusa Pacific University
Azusa, California

"In *Partners in Ministry*, Jim skillfully and clearly elaborates on the calling of every Christian to ministry, the role of pastors as enablers, and how each, being what the Lord intended, not only edifies the Church, but also lives out a mission to the world. This book is well-written and very practical. Pastors and laypeople alike will find in these pages a challenge for the Church to truly become an army of ministers—equipped to serve in Jesus' name."

Steve Riggle, Senior Pastor
Grace Community Church
Houston, Texas

"Dr. Garlow has (through scriptural exposition and research) made the universal call to ministry of all Christians unequivocal. As laity accepts the fact that pastor and church members are separated by function, not by essence, the concept of partnership in ministry becomes appealing. The book is refreshing in its approach, easy to comprehend yet challenging and practical in the talk of equipping. Dr. Garlow's sensitivity to those he shepherds is illustrated in his awareness of their personal priorities, the necessity of training, and putting support groups in place to share and encourage, and direction given to identify gifts of individual believers."

Dr. Paul Mills, President
Bartlesville Wesleyan College
Bartlesville, Oklahoma

PARTNERS

IN

MINISTRY

PARTNERS

IN

MINISTRY

LAITY AND PASTORS WORKING TOGETHER

JAMES L. GARLOW

Beacon Hill Press of Kansas City
Kansas City, Missouri

Copyright 1981, 1998
Beacon Hill Press of Kansas City
Second Edition 1998

ISBN 083-410-6930

Printed in the
United States of America

Diagrams by MJ Graphics

Library of Congress Catalog Card Number 81-146332

10   9   8   7   6   5   4   3   2

Dedicated to
two laypersons who taught me
by their lives
that they were ministers—
my parents:
Burtis Garlow, farmer; Winifred Garlow, housewife

Contents

Preface 19

About the Author 20

Introduction 21

1 / The Biblical Basis 23

2 / A Look at the Theology 31

3 / What History Tells Us 51

4 / Our Gifts for Ministry 68

5 / Training for Ministry 85

6 / Sent into Ministry 109

Appendix A—From Discovering My Gift to
Finding My Ministry 123

Appendix B—Definitions of Gifts 130

Reference Notes 133

Preface

If you are a Christian, you are a minister. Whether or not you are ordained, Jesus Christ has called you to a meaningful ministry. Every layperson is called to ministry.

This concept is not new; it is new only to us. It is not new to many thinkers throughout the history of the Christian Church. It is not new to the writers of Scripture. And it is least of all new to God himself, for that is the way He designed it. The concept of the ministry of the laity may seem new to us because this truth has been underemphasized in the past. From all appearances, however, it is being reclaimed in our present time. I believe we are part of a movement. Indeed, we are part of a revolution. A revolution of liberation is taking place—the liberation of the laity.

This revolution will liberate laypersons to become more fully what they already are—ministers in the biblical sense. The coming liberation is not a liberation *from* something but a liberation *to* something—to ministry or service. The revolution is not here yet. But I do hear the sounds of its coming; if you will listen with me, I think you will hear them too. Howard Butt notes, "Across the past few years institutes and programs produced by or urging lay assertivism have flowered like violets in spring. . . . What is happening . . . is a widening and deepening of the laity's understanding of the Christian responsibility."[1] Carlyle Marney wrote of the inevitability of the coming revolution: "It is morally certain that some change is on the way, something like the changes that occurred during the Luther-Calvin-Zwingli-Wesley times."[2]

Elton Trueblood, often regarded as the grandfather of the lay ministry movement, states it most powerfully when he writes, "If the average church should suddenly take seriously the notion that every laymember—man or woman—is really a minister of Christ, we could have something like a revolution in a very short time."[3] Dr. Thomas Gillespie, president of Princeton Theological Seminary, warns that the revolution "will be realized only if the 'nonclergy' are willing to move up, if the 'clergy' are willing to move over, and if all God's people are willing to move out."[4]

We are living in exciting times. We are on the verge of a meaningful reclamation of the heritage that every believer is truly called to ministry. You are a participant in that revolution. Whether you are a pastor or a layperson, you have the joyful responsibility of responding to the call to ministry that comes to every believer.

Join me in the revolution.

—JAMES L. GARLOW

About the Author

Dr. James L. Garlow is senior pastor of Skyline Wesleyan Church, a congregation of over 3,000 in average attendance, located in San Diego, California. Prior to that Dr. Garlow has served as a church planter in the Dallas-Fort Worth area and an associate pastor in Oklahoma City. He is a graduate of Bartlesville Wesleyan College (A.A.), Southern Nazarene University (B.A. and M.A.), Asbury Theological Seminary (M.Div.), Princeton Theological Seminary (M.Th.), and Drew University (Ph.D.). His doctoral dissertation was titled "John Wesley's Understanding of the Laity as Demonstrated by His Use of the Lay Preachers." He and his wife, Carol, have four children: Janie, Joshua, Jacob, and Josie.

Introduction

Lay ministry has been a significant part of my life for portions of four decades. In the late 1960s, while a college sophomore, I listened to Dr. D. James Kennedy preach a sermon on Eph. 4:11-12. I was riveted as he stated that the role of pastors was to equip and mobilize laity for ministry rather than doing all of the ministry themselves. Admittedly, that is not a radical concept today, but it certainly was to me then. I was so excited about his sermon that I bought the reel-to-reel tape (audiocassettes were uncommon at that time) and played it over and over. I memorized portions of it and began to share the contents with other people. As a college student, I would play the tape for any fellow religion major who might be willing to listen.

During the 1970s I had the privilege of going through four graduate degrees. A major portion of my academic focus was an attempt to understand the exciting principle that laity are to be equipped and trained for the ministry rather than merely passive recipients of ministry. My doctoral dissertation was an analysis of Wesley's utilization of the laity. Wesley was severely criticized for many things, but none more than his confidence in the role of laity in carrying the gospel. As I was nearing completion of the study, I asked myself what concepts of Wesley were transferable across an ocean and across 250 years. I discovered that from Wesley's perspective, laity are *called* to ministry, *gifted* for ministry, to be *trained* for ministry, and *sent* into ministry.

The 1980s provided me an opportunity to write, speak, and experiment in the area of lay ministry. I began the decade by writing the L.I.T.E. (Lay Institute to Equip) manual. Close on the heels of that was the *Partners in Ministry* book, which you now hold in your hand. In addition to that I had the privilege of speaking on the topic in numerous locations, which helped to further refine my thinking. I wrote my first (and, I suspect, my only) musical, titled *We (laity) Are Ministers,* which Ken Van Wyk graciously included as part of the Lay Ministers Training Center at Robert Schuller's Crystal Cathedral in Garden Grove, California, in January of 1983. In addition, two videotapes were produced (though they were a bit ahead of their time, since no one had VCRs at home yet) titled *Partners in Ministry* and *All God's People,* which was a review of the theology of the laity of six key figures of church history: St. Francis, Martin Luther, John Wesley, Alexander Campbell, John R. Mott, and Pope John XXIII.

During the early part of the 1980s I had the privilege of serving in a megachurch (in the Oklahoma City area) as an associate pastor with the unique title of minister of lay development. It allowed me to experiment in various ways of training and equipping laity for the ministry. By the mid-1980s I had planted a church in Dallas-Fort Worth and was further experimenting how to equip and mobilize laity for ministry.

In the 1990s I am now a senior pastor in a large church in Southern California, but the importance of lay ministry has not diminished at all. As I prepare this new edition of *Partners in Ministry,* I am launching an extensive one-year lay ministry training program involving nearly 600 of the approximately 3,100 Sunday morning attenders.

As a college student in the 1960s, lay ministry was an exciting concept. In the 1970s it was a fascinating motivation for my graduate studies. In the 1980s it provided an opportunity to write, teach, and experiment. During the 1990s I have become even more convinced of its importance. It is an absolute necessity. We will not—we cannot—impact the world for Christ the way we want to unless *all God's people* are equipped and trained for the exciting ministry to which God has called them.

If you are reading this as a layperson, I pray that you will understand the tremendous importance you play in the kingdom of God. You are not a second-class citizen. You are called by Almighty God to ambassadorial status. If you are reading this as a pastor, I pray that it will encourage you to continue to train the laity around you, mobilizing them as a mighty force for Christ.

JIM GARLOW
San Diego, California

1
The Biblical Basis

Layperson, you are something special. You are important to God and to the growth of His exciting kingdom. It's apparent to most of us that "God must have loved the layperson since he made so many of them."[1] Did it ever occur to you that most of the people who follow Jesus Christ are laypersons? In any given congregation in America, all but one or two or three of the persons in that congregation are laypersons.

Unfortunately, most laypeople are unemployed—in the kingdom of Christ, that is. Some have suggested that perhaps as many as 95 percent of God's people are unemployed. So critical is this situation that laypersons have occasionally been defined as the unemployed of the church. God did not intend it that way. And it was not that way in the beginning days of the New Testament Church.

A. *Paul's Five Preparatory Ministries*

God's Word has something to say to us in this area. In Ephesians we read, "It was he who gave some to be apostles, some to be prophets, some to be evangelists, and some to be pastors and teachers, to prepare God's people for works of service, so that the body of Christ may be built up" (4:11-12). The apostles, prophets, evangelists, pastors, and teachers have an exciting role to fill. It is described in verse 12. It is essentially one task. What is that task? The task is to equip God's people, *all believers*, for the work of *ministry*. Their ministry then *strengthens* the Church.

The ministries given by Christ to His Church have a common purpose—to prepare God's people for the work of ministry.

Whether pastor, evangelist, or teacher, the primary task is to equip others to share in the ministry. As a pastor, my primary assignment is to train others for their respective ministries. I am to be an equipper. The major task of the seminary is not just to produce the professional clergy but to train those who can train *others* for *their* ministries.

Some translations of Eph. 4:12 place a comma after the word "saints," making three phrases: "For the perfecting of the saints, for the work of the ministry, for the edifying of the body of Christ" (KJV). These three phrases, then, appear to indicate three different tasks of a pastor, teacher, or prophet: (1) to perfect the saints, (2) to do the work of ministry, (3) to edify the Body of Christ.

The Clergy Have Three Tasks:

1. *Perfect the Saints*
2. *Work of ministry*
3. *edify the body of Christ*

...or do they?

The "Enablers" Have One Task:

*equip God's people
for service / Ministry
to strengthen the
Church*

Many translations do not place a comma between the words "saints" and "for." These commas tend to alter the meaning of the verse. Hans-Ruedi Weber refers to this punctuation as "the fateful comma" because it so significantly alters the intent of the verse. If we maintain the comma in verse 12, the ministry mentioned there appears to be something done by the pastors, teachers, and so on. This rules out ministry done by *all believers.* It limits ministry to a select few. This passage, properly understood, tells us that *all God's people* are to be prepared for ministry. It is this crucial involvement of *all* believers that produces growth in the Church of Jesus Christ.

The word "prepare" in verse 12 (NIV) is sometimes translated "equip," "complete," or "perfect." Its first occurrence in the Greek New Testament is in connection with the calling of several followers of Christ. As Jesus was walking along the Sea of Galilee, He invited two sets of brothers—Peter and Andrew, James and John—to follow Him. These brothers were in their boats mending their nets. The word translated "mending" is the same word translated "equipping" or "preparing" in Eph. 4:12.

What does that say to us? It tells us that the process that the nets were going through under the supervision of those Galilean fishermen is comparable to the process that we go through under the supervision of our Lord. Those nets were being equipped; so are we. They were being fixed; so are we. They were being prepared for the purpose for which they were intended; so are we. We are under construction, being fitted out for our respective works of ministry.

B. *Peter's Six Meaningful Terms*

The apostle Peter joins Paul in stressing that all the people of God, not just the professional clergy, are ministers. In 1 Pet. 2:4-5, 9-10, he writes: "Come to him, the living Stone—rejected by men but chosen by God and precious to him—you also, like living stones, are being built into a spiritual house to be a holy priesthood, offering spiritual sacrifices acceptable to God through Jesus Christ. . . . But you are a chosen people, a royal priesthood, a holy nation, a people belonging to God, that you may declare the praises of him who called you out of darkness into his wonderful light. Once you were not a people, but now you are the people of God; once you had not received mercy, but now you have received mercy."

Peter used six terms in these verses to describe the followers of Jesus Christ. In the TEV, the first one is the phrase "living stones"; the second one, "holy priests"; the third, "chosen race"; the fourth, "King's priests"; the fifth, "holy nation"; and the last, "God's own people."

The first term that describes us as followers of Jesus Christ is "living stones." The question is: If we are "living stones," in what way are we to be used? What is our service or ministry? Jesus is the Cornerstone in an ongoing construction project—the building of the Kingdom. We, too, have been selected, regardless of all our inadequacies, to be living stones, to be a part of the same building in which Christ has been used. Look around you right now. You may not see it; you may not even hear it. But there is a construction project underway greater than humankind can possibly fathom. And you and I, as followers of Jesus Christ, are a part of that project.

In verse 5, we are called priests; we are even called "holy priests." What is a priest? A priest is someone who offers up something to God. What do we offer to God? Ourselves. As followers of Jesus Christ we are priests, daily offering up ourselves to God in service and ministry. We, as holy priests, offer up all that we have, all that we can become, to Him. That is one of the ways in which we can function as holy priests.

In verses 9 and 10, we learn that we are a part of a chosen race. And then—can we believe it?—it says we are among "the King's priests" (TEV). We're not simply anybody's priests; we are priests of the King! Sovereign King of the entire universe! What an honor! We belong to the "royal priesthood." Then we are members of a "holy nation." And finally, we are "God's own people" (TEV).

Why were we so fortunate? Why have we been chosen? We have been chosen so that we can make known the wonderful, redemptive acts of God. This is the ministry of the laity. This is the ministry of each of us. All of us are especially chosen by God as being valuable to Him. We are part of a special Kingdom, a special nation of people, and we have been set apart for a crucial ministry.

In his book titled *Everyone a Minister*, Oscar Feucht states, "These titles raise all believers to the status of 'minister.' They put all Christians in the role once performed by Old Testament priests."[2] Thomas Gillespie writes, "This is the new *upward* direction which a biblical perspective on the laity requires of us—the elevation of every member of God's people to the status of a minister."[3]

The apostle Peter selected significant words to convey his

message. For example, the word "temple" refers to that which is being built within us, the kingdom of God. As one writer noted, "God's 'dwelling place' on earth is no longer conceived of as a building set apart from the world but as a people set in and sent unto the world."[4] In his letter to the Ephesian Christians, Paul writes about this temple: "Consequently, you are no longer foreigners and aliens, but fellow citizens with God's people and members of God's household, built on the foundation of the apostles and prophets, with Christ Jesus himself as the chief cornerstone. In him the whole building is joined together and rises to become a holy temple in the Lord. And in him you too are being built together to become a dwelling in which God lives by his Spirit" (2:19-22).

A second word the apostle Peter uses in his first letter has significance for our discussion. It is the word "priest." Who is a priest? *All believers* are priests. There was a time in biblical history when the priesthood was limited to the descendants of Aaron. Not so in the New Testament. The Book of Hebrews tells us that the Old Testament rites were temporary and that a day would come when a new priesthood would be formed. That day has come! We are that priesthood!

Another word we need to understand in its New Testament meaning is the term "sacrifice." The New Testament does not end sacrifices, but it surely changes the nature of the sacrifices. The sacrifice called for in the New Testament is ourselves. Paul says that we give our bodies, meaning all our activities, everything we have, as a sacrifice for Him (Rom. 12:1). Our sacrifices may include such things as praise and thanksgiving, personal confession, loving service, or deeds done in the spirit of love. All of these comprise ministry. That is what is called for from us as priests. We are to make sacrifices that are acceptable and pleasing to God. Hans Küng observes that "these offerings are not part of worship in a sanctuary, but worship in the world, in the middle of everyday life, the loving service of God. . . . This is the true sacrifice of the New Testament priesthood."[5]

C. *No New Concept*

The concept of the ministry of all of God's people is not limited to the New Testament. At Mount Sinai God instructed Moses regarding the ministry of ancient Israel. He said:

"This is what you are to say to the house of Jacob and what you are to tell the people of Israel: 'You yourselves have seen what I did to Egypt, and how I carried you on eagles' wings and brought you to myself. Now if you obey me fully and keep my covenant, then out of all nations you will be my treasured possession. Although the whole earth is mine, you will be for me a kingdom of priests and a holy nation.' These are the words you are to speak to the Israelites."

So Moses went back and summoned the elders of the people and set before them all the words the LORD had commanded him to speak. The people all responded together, "We will do everything the LORD has said." So Moses brought their answer back to the LORD *(Exod. 19:3-8).*

In verse 6 God calls the children of Israel "a kingdom of priests." He is not referring simply to those in the professional priesthood. He is saying that Israel as a nation—as a people—was called to service, was called to ministry. They had what Thomas Gillespie has called a "mediating ministry," that is, standing between God and the world. All the Israelites were called to this important ministry. Certainly they were called as a nation, but this did not diminish the role of each individual within that nation.

Israel's problem was that they became confused about their call. They did not understand that they were called, not to *status* or to *honor* or to a position of *privilege,* but rather to *servanthood* or *ministry.* God's original dream was that His people would function as a kingdom of priests standing between Him and a world needing to know about Him. The prophet Isaiah reminds us that "you will be called priests of the LORD, you will be named ministers of our God" (61:6). The fulfillment of this ancient dream is occurring today in the Church. It is occurring now in us. We are all ministers.

We discover this same truth in the last book of the Bible. John tells us that Christ "loves us and has freed us from our sins by his blood, and has made us to be a kingdom and priests to serve his God and Father" (Rev. 1:5-6). Note also what the Revelator says on this same theme in 5:9-10 and 20:6. Oscar Feucht wrote, "It is unmistakably clear that the term 'Priest" as used in the New Testament does not refer to officiants in a church building but describes *all Christians* in their role as the priesthood of all believers."[6] James Reston, at a press conference at the Congress on the Laity in Los Angeles, stated, "Religion is too serious a business to be left to the clergy."[7] Someone has pointed out that Christianity is different from a football game. Football has been described as "22 men on the field who desperately need rest and 16,000 people in the stands who desperately need exercise." Contrary to popular opinion, *Christianity is not a spectator sport.* Every believer is a minister! Everyone is involved.

Now you may be saying, "I'm just a layperson." If so, Francis Ayers' words may be for you: "You are a minister of Christ . . . if you are a baptized Christian, you are already a minister, whether you are ordained or not is immaterial. No matter how you react, the statement remains true. You may be surprised, alarmed, pleased, antagonized, suspicious, acquiescent, scornful, or enraged. Nevertheless you are a minister of Christ."[8]

I am a minister. Let's make that our quote for the day. Jesse Jackson, a strong spokesman for the civil rights movement, came to national notoriety through Operation Breadbasket. He has a unique ability to motivate a crowd. He'll stand before an African American high school student body and say, "Repeat after me: I am—somebody!" And then the crowd responds, "I am—somebody!" He leads the crowd in other cheers such as "Up with hope; down with dope." And the crowd roars back, "Up with hope; down with dope." As I watched how enthusiastic his audience became from hearing him speak, I realized we could learn something from him. It might be good for some of us to say, "I am a minister! I am a living stone! I am a holy priest! I am a part of the chosen race! I am one of the King's priests! I am part of a holy nation! I am one of God's own people!"

I've ended several of my lay ministry training sessions by having the laypersons say: "I am a minister. . . . I am a priest. . . ." Layperson, it may feel awkward at first, but you should refer to yourself as a minister. Why? Because that's what you are, or at least want to become.

Layperson, pastor, you are both ministers. God has called you to serve Him, to share His love with others. As laity and pastors, we are partners in ministry.

Discussion Questions

1. For the layperson, what is the practical significance of the following expressions from 1 Pet. 2:4-5, 9-10?

    a. "living stones"

    b. "a holy priesthood"

    c. "a chosen people"

    d. "a holy nation"

    e. "the people of God"

2. What is the purpose of the designated ministries as outlined in Eph. 4:11-12?

3. What is the meaning of the expression "living sacrifice" as found in Rom. 12:1?

4. How does maturity in Christ contribute to the effectiveness of the ministry of the laity?

5. Discuss the following ideas:

    a. God never intended that the total ministry of His kingdom should be the sole responsibility of the professional pastors.

    b. The idea of the involvement of the laity in Kingdom building is both an Old and New Testament concept.

    c. Christianity is not a spectator sport.

    d. The word "priest" must be applied to all believers and not just to the ordained ministers.

    e. The increased involvement of the laity in ministry is one of the most hopeful signs of the latter part of the 20th century.

2
A Look at the Theology

"But I'm not a theologian," you may say. But to some extent all believers are theologians. The word "theology" comes from two Greek words: *theos*, which means "God"; and *logia*, which means "the study of." Theology is simply the study of God. And every sincere believer has a desire to know more about God. So in a sense, all of us are theologians—admittedly amateur theologians many times—but still theologians of sorts. Even the simplest of comments like "Jesus is Lord" is a theological statement. Thus in a very real sense we are all involved in the process known as theology.

Theology is broad in scope with major areas of concern. For example, *Christology* is the study of Christ. *Soteriology* is the study of salvation. *Hamartiology* pertains to the doctrine of sin. *Eschatology* is the doctrine of the last times. *Ecclesiology* is the study of the Church. It is under this last important branch of theology that the ministry of the laity falls.

Much of what we do is determined by what we believe. For example, I believe the engine on my car will start if I insert the key and turn the ignition. I believe if I put the car into drive, it will begin to move forward. If I did not believe these things, I would not do them. So it is with the ministry of the laity. If I believe that there is such a thing as a ministry of the laity and I have a place for it in my thinking, I will want to do certain things.

Perhaps it can be best illustrated this way: If I believe that our pastor is *the* minister and I am not a minister, I will not get involved in ministry. On the other hand, if I conceive of myself

31

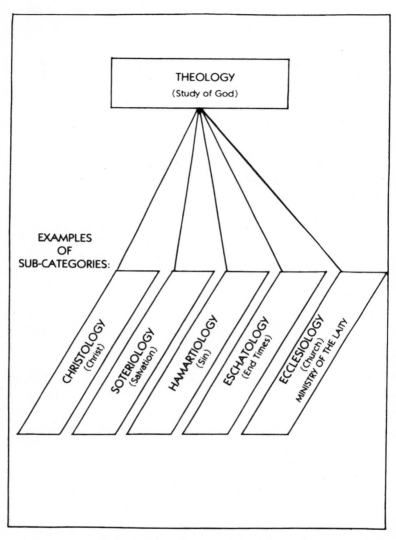

as being a minister along with my pastor, I will get involved in ministry. The way we think about certain things causes us to respond to them in certain ways. Thus it is important for us to have a theology of lay ministry. If we have a clear theology of lay ministry, we should be well on our way to responding like lay ministers should.

We are not concerned with a theology *for* the laity but rather with a theology *of* the laity or a theology *about* the laity. A theology *for* the laity would simply mean taking any kind of theological talk, whatever it might be about, and translating it into lay terminology. That's not our concern here. There is plenty of that kind of material available. Our concern is not simply to make theology palatable for laypersons. Our concern is different. We want to make sure that we all have in our minds a theology that includes the important place of the layperson. This is what we mean by a theology *of* the laity or *about* the laity, not merely theology *for* laypersons. Possibly in your past the word "theology" has tended to put you to sleep. It sounded boring. We believe you will find a *theology of the laity* to be the opposite—very exciting.

What does a theology of the ministry of the laity involve? It's really not as complex as we might think. We can understand it by taking a closer look at four words: (1) church, (2) ministry, (3) laity, and (4) vocation.

I. CHURCH

What is a church? If you were to list all of the things needed to have a church, what would you write on your list? Would you include an organ, a piano, a pulpit, pews, stained-glass windows, a steeple topped with a cross, offering plates?

During the Middle Ages, the question was sometimes asked, "What is a church?" Some of the theologians of the time answered it by saying the church was the hierarchy or the clergy. The way to define a church, according to them, was the clergy. Martin Luther, writing in the 1500s, reacted against that definition. Surely the clergy do not fully describe a church. In order to have a church, Luther believed the following must be present: (1) the Word being rightly preached, and (2) the sacraments being properly administered. John Calvin, writing a bit later than Luther, added a third thing to the list. He noted that Christians are a disciplined people. Not only must we have the preached Word and the sacraments, but we also must have discipline present to have a church.

Throughout history other things have been added to the list. I would like to suggest that for us to have a church, we need to

To Have A "Church" One Must Have

A Ministry of the Laity

CHURCH: (definition)

1. PRE████G
2. SA█████NTS
3. DIS█████

4. Mutual Ministry

add mutual ministry. In other words, the marks of a true church are the preached Word, the sacraments being properly administered, evidences of discipline, and finally, ministry. By that I mean ministry that occurs within the body or within the fellowship. Hendrik Kraemer wrote, "The church, well-understood, not so much *has* a ministry or ministries, but primarily *is* a ministry."[1] What are we saying? The church, if it is to be understood as the New Testament portrays it, is *ministry*.

II. Ministry

The area of theology that best describes the role of the church is *ecclesiology*, or the doctrine of the church. If we are to have a proper theological system that includes laypeople, many of us need to rework our ecclesiology. As one person put it, "We will find the amazing fact that, notwithstanding the often great, even crucial significance of the laity, they have never become really theologically relevant in the church's thinking about itself. Therefore, in raising today the lay issue in the church, one raises at the same time the demand for a new ecclesiology (doctrine of the church)."[2] So the reason we are giving attention to our understanding of the church is because that is where our theology of the laity must fit. The church is ministry, and properly understood, one of the distinguishing marks of the church is ministry occurring within itself—being done *by* and *for* its members.

From where does the church derive its ministry? From whom did it receive this important calling? How does it know what ministry is? Ministry, in the New Testament, is derived from Christ. As Richard Harrington described it, "The church *is* ministry. In fact, in order for the church to be the authentic representative of Jesus Christ, it *must* be ministry because Jesus established a ministry, not a church."[3]

Jesus made the meaning of ministry clear. He told it simply. He "did not come to be served, but to serve" (Mark 10:45). It is interesting that the Greek term from which we get the word "ministry" is *diakonia*, which usually means "to serve." Jesus declared, "Whosoever wants to become great among you must be your servant, and whoever wants to be first must be your slave" (Matt. 20:26-27). In simple terms, ministry equals servanthood.

A. *In the Church*

The ministry that Jesus began did not end at the time of His ascension. The fact is it continues in us. William Barclay notes, "Acts is the second volume of the story which has no end. The gospel was only the story of what Jesus *began* to do and to teach. Jesus' earthly life was only the beginning of an activity which knows no end."[4] You and I have the amazing privilege of carrying on precisely what Jesus began. Martin Luther explained it most directly with these words, "You are a *little Christ.*"

Two thousand years ago, God become man in the person of Jesus. This event is called the Incarnation. What does the word *carne* mean? In some languages, such as Spanish, it refers to "meat." In other languages it refers to "flesh." "Incarnation" simply means the "en-flesh-ment" of God. God himself chose to take on human flesh and to minister within those confines. In one sense the Incarnation continues today. God continues to dwell in human flesh—in His Body, the Body of Christ, the Church. We acknowledge the uniqueness of Christ's incarnation. At the same time it is important to acknowledge that sense in which the Incarnation continues in you and me. "It is the whole lesson of the book of Acts that the life of Jesus goes on *in His* church."[5]

Jesus is not physically present in the way He once was, but the Spirit of God continues His ministry through us. As one writer notes, "Jesus did not only leave an immortal name and influence; He is still alive and still active and still powerful. He is not the One who *was;* He is the One who *is* and His life still goes on."[6] We might refer to all this as *incarnational theology.* Incarnational theology means this: when we reach out and touch other people, *it is not we who actually touch, but Christ who touches through us.* As we begin to touch others in our ministry, we discover that the hand touching them is not our own. It is the hand of Christ. The Incarnation, in this sense, continues on in us. The omnipotent, omniscient, omnipresent God chooses, for reasons inexplicable, to work through us.

This truth is stated most powerfully in a musical titled *The Gathering,* written by Ken Medema. It states:

> When the church is the church, it is nothing more or less or other than the presence of Christ through His people.
>
> A part of the meaning of grace is that Christ is in us for each other. We are called to be priests to each other.
>
> If we are the church, then I may come to you as I may come to Christ . . . just as I am, knowing that you will understand my tears, my anger, my sin, believing that somehow Christ will see with your eyes, touch me with your hands, heal me with your love.*

If we want to see the living Christ today, we need to look to our brothers and sisters. They are His representatives. They are, in fact, those who continue that which Jesus began. If we want to see the ministry of Jesus, we must look around. In fact, we can look into the mirror!

When we reach out to touch another life, in our act of continuing this ministry of Christ, we find ourselves reaching, first, within the church. We reach specifically to those who are a part of the fellowship of the Body of Christ. It is quite proper for us to use the word "priest" not merely as a noun but also as a verb. I "priest" you and you "priest" me. We function as priests to each other.

The Gathering by Ken Medema. © Copyright 1977 by Word Music, Inc. (A Div. of Word, Inc.). All Rights Reserved. International Copyright Secured. Used by Permission.

B. *In the World*

There is a second direction that we reach when we attempt to continue the ministry of Christ. We reach not only within the Church but also outside the Church into the world. A popular song of a number of years ago went, "Reach out and touch somebody's hand, / And make this world a better place if you can." I think we can improve on that by altering those words ever so slightly—"Reach out and touch somebody's hand. / Make this world a better place—yes, He can!" What are we saying? Who reaches out? We do. But who actually touches the life? He does. He touches through us.

The Eternal Lord inhabits our lives and those around us through our actions and our caring for others. That is what lay ministry is all about: God at work in the lives of His people. That is what Roger Copeland wrote about in the song titled "Reach Out to Your Neighbor."

Reach out to your neighbor, let him know you really care.
Reach out when he's lonely, let him know somebody's there.
Reach out in his darkness when the clouds obscure his view.
Just walk with him and talk with him, he's waiting for you.

1. *Salt*

Jesus told a group of His followers they were to be "the salt of the earth" (Matt. 5:13). What did He mean by that? Salt, to those who were listening to Jesus, had several meanings. First, salt was *pure*. Christ was instructing those who followed Him that their lives should reflect a quality of purity. Second, salt was a *preservative*. Some of you can remember the day before modern refrigeration, when salt was used to preserve meat. To the Greek mind, salt gave meat a new soul.

Third, salt flavored. We so appreciate the flavoring capability of salt that we often reach for the saltshaker when we sit down to a meal.

A fourth quality of salt—and for our purposes an important quality—is that it makes people *thirsty*. My favorite food is popcorn. I would rather have a bowl (a big one!) of popcorn than a thick steak. When I am away from home for a few days, I try to work popcorn into the conversation so my host or hostess will understand that I will have withdrawal pains if I'm not served my favorite delicacy! With popcorn always comes thirst. Why? Is it the butter? No. Is it the popcorn itself? No. It is the salt. Salt creates thirst. Your life as a lay minister creates thirst in those around you—thirst for the Living Water. When Jesus said, "You are the salt of the earth," He meant that we are to have a certain attractiveness about us. It will create a desire for what we have as believers. It will cause people to question us. This will create opportunities to give a reason for the hope that lies within us.

2. *Light*

Jesus also told His followers, "You are the light of the world" (v. 14). By this He meant first that as believers we are to be *visible,* to be seen. There is no such thing as secret discipleship, no Christian in isolation from the world. I once heard about a Christian building contractor who wanted to build a city that would be inhabited only by Christians. I am glad the project failed because it would be a misunderstanding of our New Testament calling for believers to associate only with other believers. The truth is *we are most the Church when we are not in the church building!*

We need to understand another quality about light. Light is a *guide.* There are times when followers of Christ serve as guides to the world. This is not at all surprising when we consider the fact that the world does not have a long-term purpose for living. As believers we are involved in a movement considerably bigger than ourselves that will outlast ourselves.

A third quality about light that applies to us as believers is that light sometimes gives *warning,* like a lighthouse. In that same way, those who follow Christ, by the very character of their holy lives, stand in silent judgment upon the world, warning it of its own self-destruction.

3. *Outreach*

There is a danger to which we need to be alert. Churches can become so ingrown and self-contained that they lose all contact with those who most need to hear their message. This might be called saltshaker Christianity. It is often easier for us to stay in the saltshaker than it is for us to be dispersed. Certainly there is a proper time for the *church gathered.* But the church gathers only so that it can receive strength to be *scattered.* Donald McGavran, father of the church growth movement, sounds this warning: "It is true that churches can so divorce themselves from their neighbors that, sealed off and introverted, they cannot communicate the gospel. They have disobeyed the Bible and taken themselves out of the world. Christians must remain in the world. Like their Master, they become incarnate in the ignorant, filthy, and sinful villages and cities of their real world."[7]

The Church and The World

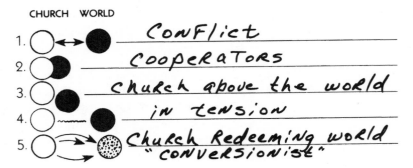

CHURCH   WORLD

1. Conflict
2. Cooperators
3. Church above the world
4. in tension
5. Church Redeeming world
   "Conversionist"

The reason for the existence of the church is so that it may focus as the redeeming force on those who still remain outside its borders. H. Richard Niebuhr notes that there are five different ways of describing the relationship between Christ and culture. One way of understanding the relationship between the church and contemporary culture is that they are *at odds with one another*. They have conflicting value systems. A second way of understanding them is to see them as *the same*. Some people would perceive the church and the world to be cooperators with each other. A third way of viewing the relationship between the church and its environment is to perceive of the church as somehow being *above culture*—superior to it and aloof from it. A fourth way of perceiving this relationship is to see them as always being *in tension* with one another. According to this view, both are necessary, yet they are never quite reconciled to each other. There is one more description of the relationship between the church and culture. This fifth perception sees the church as the *transformer of culture*. This is referred to as the conversionist view. This simply means that the church, properly conceived, is in the process of bringing about the redemption of all society.

Clifford Wright has illustrated this redemptive role in the following three diagrams. First of all, he notes that Christians are *called into the Church from the world.* In other words, they are *gath-*

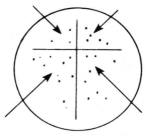

ered. Second, believers are then *sent into the world.* They are *scattered;* they are to bring others back *into the Church.* Finally, Christians are *sent out, scattered* once again. They are scattered for the

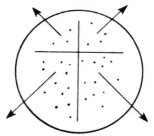

purpose of transforming society. Those persons sent out by Christ are sent not merely to extract others from the swamp (evangelism) but also to clean up the swamp. The ministry of God's people is as much in the *world* as it is in the *church.*[8]

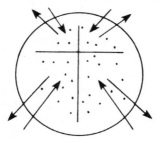

III. LAITY

Have you ever heard anyone say, "But I am just a layperson"? Anyone apologizing with "but I am just a layperson" certainly does not understand the high calling of being a layperson. How would you define a "layperson"? If you were to write out a definition, what would you include? I have asked that question of many people. Do you know what they answered? Yes, you've already figured it out, haven't you? When I have asked people to write out a definition for layperson, they almost always put down, "A layperson is one who is not a preacher, who hasn't gone to seminary, and who is not a reverend." Now that is an incredibly inadequate definition. It is seldom useful to define something by what it is *not*. Rather, we should define something by what it *is*. For example, if I ask you to give me a definition of a banana, you would not say, "Well, a banana is not made out of steel, it is not 40 stories tall, and it does not have a CB radio." Well, then, how do we define *laity?*

A. *"Laikos" or "Laos"?*

The Greek language has two words from which we derive the term "laity." One is *laikos;* the other is *laos. Laikos* means layperson in the sense of uneducated masses, a person who is not a specialist, who knows little about the subject matter. In contrast to that, *laos* means "people." In the New Testament it generally means "the people of God." It is important to note that the word *laikos* ("uneducated masses") never appears in the New Testament. In contrast, the New Testament repeatedly uses the word *laos* ("people of God"). In other words, when you find yourself admitting, "But I am just a layperson," you might as well say, "I am just *one of the people of God."* By saying this, we change the meaning of layperson from something negative and empty to something rich in its biblical and historical understanding. What a powerful compliment it is to be one of the people of God! We who are followers of Christ are a part of the *laos,* the people of God. The next time you hear someone say, "Oh, but I am just a layperson," congratulate him or her on the tremendous honor of being one of God's people.

Let's go a step further with this word "ministry." If we were to write a theological statement concerning ministry, what would it include? Ordinarily when people think of the ministry, they think immediately in terms of preachers, clergy, seminary-trained persons. Anytime one hears the word "minister" on television or radio or in a newspaper, it invariably refers to those who are officially recognized ordained persons. But that is not a biblical use of that term. A proper understanding of ministry must begin with the ministry of *all believers*—the ministry of the *laos,* all of God's people. This is sometimes referred to as the common ministry or the universal ministry. It means that all of us as followers of Christ have been called to service or ministry in the name of Christ.

Within that body of people, the *laos,* is a group of people who we call the clergy. They are sometimes referred to as the specialized ministry or the representative ministry. In other words, *all believers are called to minister. All Christians, biblically considered, are ministers.* Any understanding of the ministry must start with that affirmation. Beyond that, there are those within the total Body of Christ who have been called and trained for a specialized area of service. These we might refer to as our pastors or the clergy.

What is the role of those with such a specialized ministry? Well, certainly teaching or preaching the Word has priority. Then there is the administering of the sacraments—baptism and the Lord's Supper. Another function of the specialized ministry is the administration of church life for the sake of order. If everyone saw himself or herself as being in charge, church life would be utter chaos. But for the sake of a meaningful and effective operation, we understand that certain persons within our group are administrators. A fourth function that seems to be important is *enablement.* By that we mean making it possible for all God's people to minister. For the ordained clergy, one of the most important functions is *the ministry of enablement.* That means helping and assisting laypersons with their respective ministries. Some within the clergy best fulfill their call to minister when they enable others to minister. It is for this reason that pastors have a specialized or enabling ministry within the universal ministry.

How should we write a statement on the ministry? One group of people wrote it as follows: "Section One—The Nature of Ministry—ministry in the Christian church is derived from the ministry of Christ. . . . It is a ministry bestowed upon and re-

quired of the entire church. All Christians are called to ministry
. . . Section Two—The Ordained Ministry—There are persons
within the ministry of the baptized who are called of God and
set apart by the church for the specialized ministry of Word,
sacrament, and order."[9] In other words, any discussion about
ministry must begin with the ministry of the laity, if it is to be
biblically valid.

B. *Who Are the Ministers?*

The following diagrams may be helpful in clarifying the
New Testament concept of ministry. The first two diagrams illustrated common but unbiblical perceptions of the laity. The third
diagram illustrates what we have been stating in the previous
pages. Let's look at the first diagram. Some people would view
the clergy and laity as totally separate. They envision that God
has called certain people to be ministers and certain people to be
laypersons, and the two are forever segregated. Other persons
would diagram the difference between clergy and laity as in fig-
ure 2. The small arrows represent ministry. Thus, laypersons receive the ministry of the ministers, ordained clergy. According to
this diagram laypersons are essentially passive. They are to *receive* ministry rather than to be *involved in* ministry.

The third diagram is the one that most closely denotes the
phrase "the ministry of the laity." In this diagram you see the arrow coming down from God. That arrow denotes a call to service
or to ministry. It is universal; it comes to all people. Every follower of Jesus Christ is called to ministry. Out of that group of
people, there are certain ones who will be part of the representative ministry. Thus, you see the arrow at the lower part of the diagram. This arrow indicates that some of the "universally called"
will be directed to become equippers (pastors). These are known
as the representative or specialized ministry. They have a unique
function in *their* ministry to the total Body of Christ.

Too often we conceive of ministry as that which is done by
the clergy. To the extent we view it that way, laypersons will be
deprived of the calling that is theirs. It would probably be better
for us if we were not to refer to those who are ordained as *the*
ministers but rather as pastors or pastoral ministers. If we take
seriously the statement that "all believers are ministers," we
shouldn't assign the title minister to only a very small percent-

Let's diagram that statement.

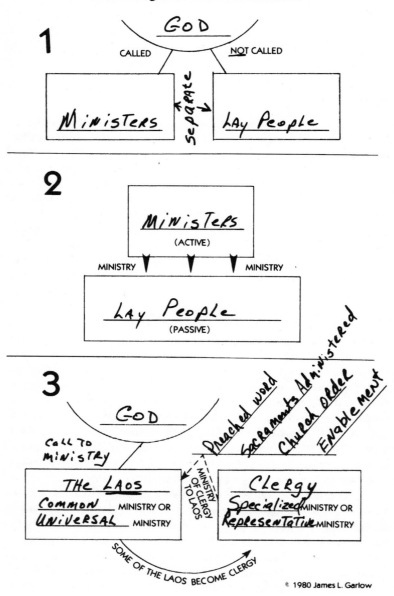

age of God's people. In a church that I previously pastored, I asked that the people never refer to me as their minister unless they were introducing me to persons that might be confused by any other title. They were to refer to me as their pastor and to see themselves as ministering laypersons. We normally used the word "ministering" to describe them as laypersons. They were reminded weekly that the church did not have *one* minister but it had as many ministers as it had followers of Christ.

There has been much confusion over the relationship of laity to the clergy. Weber diagrammed this relationship in the following manner:

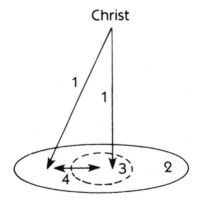

The lines pointing downward (1) represent the power of the Holy Spirit, which makes ministry possible. The larger circle (2) encompasses those known as the *church*, which includes *both* pastor and laity. The smaller circle (3), which is drawn with a dotted line, represents the set-apart ministers, who are not above the *unordained* ministers but rather among them. The relationship between pastor and laity (4) is characterized by mutual *submission* and mutual *service*.[10] This diagram portrays laity and clergy not as competitors but truly as *partners in ministry.*

Some persons mistakenly assume that this kind of emphasis negates the importance of the pastor or those we generally refer to as clergy. This is a serious misperception of what the ministry of the laity is all about. A *high doctrine of the ministry of the laity assumes an equally high doctrine of the ministry of the pastor.* Howard Grimes stated it so poignantly:

From this higher estimate of the meaning of the laity may be drawn what seems to me to be a false conclusion: namely, that ordination is of no significance, that a layman is called to do everything that a clergyman does, including even the celebration of the sacraments . . . a more adequate generalization which seems to me to draw upon the tradition within the Church, which emphasizes order with a differentiation of *function* of members. All are called by God to service; the nature of that service varies, and it included the particular work of the ordained ministry.[11]

Lay emphasis that negates the role of pastor can become lay revolt rather than lay ministry. Lay ministry needs the pastor. Albert Outler stated this in the following:

The general priesthood of all believers and the ordination of the laity do not obviate the fact that there is also a particular ministry—which I prefer to call "the representative ministry"—in the church. All organisms above the level of the amoeba differentiate their various organs and functions and exhibit a functional hierarchy. All laymen are ministers; all ministers are laymen. However, all laymen do not have the same office; and the effectiveness of the church's ministry in and for the world depends as decisively on the differentiations of various offices as on the generality of ordination and *vice versa!*[12]

Emphasis on the ministry of the laity does not negate ordination. In fact, it should make the ordination service more meaningful: One is not merely ordained to the ministry. The ordained minister is called upon to be the equipper of many ministers—lay ministers. The term "ministry" should never be reserved for those who are ordained. It belongs to the *laos*, the people of God. The terms "ministry" and "laity" cannot be separated if we desire to use them biblically.

IV. Vocation

A. *Work and Worship*

The fourth important word we consider in this discussion of ministry is *vocation*. The doctrine of vocation is sometimes paraphrased as the theology of the dust mop. What is a theology of the dust mop? Elton Trueblood said it this way: "Secular work well done is 'holy enterprise.'"[13] In other words, Monday-through-Friday work is not merely secular activity; it is an act of praise to God. Work, if we conceive of it properly, first of all, produces wholeness. It gives a sense of purpose and completeness. Workers participate in the process of creation. A proper sense of pride results from creativity. Trueblood further noted, "Work which has no other incentive than the pay check is closer to slavery than it is to freedom."[14]

Second, if we are to properly understand work, we will know that it is an extension of our worship. Worship is the act of praising God for who He is. Work is much the same. Paul said that whatever we do, we should do it for the glory of God (1 Cor. 10:31). It is quite possible to build a house or to plant corn or to perform surgery for the glory of God. It is quite possible to dust the floors as an act of praise and worship. Thus we have the theology of the dust mop. Tragically, many laypersons see their vocations as something nonreligious. Many people have allowed their employment opportunities to be "deconsecrated." By that we mean that they understand their jobs to be something quite disconnected from service to Christ.

Laypersons live a bipolar existence. They live in both the world of the church and the world of the world all at once. Persons such as myself, an ordained clergyman, live primarily in the world of the church. Not so for laypersons. They live clearly in two worlds at the same time.[15] And *what they do in both is immensely important.* A truly Christian layperson is "a garage mechanic or finisher of floors who envisages his daily work as the chief expression of the Gospel" and recognizes that "he is a partner of the living God, helping minutely in the work of Creation."[16]

B. *Double Ministry*

Laypersons have what is known as a double vocation. They have a *churchly ministry* and a *vocational ministry*. Both must be included in order to have a balanced understanding of lay ministry. If we were to talk strictly about churchly ministry without mentioning vocational ministry, laypersons might come to feel that what they do between 8 A.M. and 5 P.M. on weekdays is unimportant. This could cause people to leave their places of employment feeling the day had been wasted. They would assume that only churchly ministries are important to God.

Some churches tend to focus exclusively on one's ministry within the church structure itself. Other bodies of Christians seem to discuss only the importance of the vocational ministry. A proper understanding of the ministry of the laity requires a delicate balance. It is not either . . . or; it is both . . . and. God is immensely interested in us and our employment. Here is a hymn titled "God of Concrete, God of Steel," which speaks of this tremendous biblical doctrine:

God of concrete, God of steel, / God of piston and of wheel, / God of pylon, God of steam, / God of girder and of beam, / God of atom and of mine, / All the world of power is Thine!

Lord of table, Lord of rail, / Lord of motorway and mail, / Lord of rocket, Lord of flight, / Lord of soaring satellite, / Lord of lightning livid line, / All the world of speed is Thine!

Lord of science, Lord of art, / Lord of map and graph and chart, / Lord of physics and research, / Lord of Bible, faith and church, / Lord of sequence and design, / All the world of truth is Thine!

God, His glory fills the earth, / Gave the universe its birth, / Loosed the Christ with Easter's might, / Saved the world with evil blight, / Claims mankind by grace divine, / All the world of love is Thine!

One of the avenues of ministry is our vocation. The very acts that we perform in our vocation are, *in and of themselves, ministry.* In other words, when my father goes out to the field to plant corn, the act of planting corn itself is a ministry to society at large that is every bit as important to God as the time I spend preparing a sermon. God is no less interested in how we paint a house or how we wash the dishes than He is in how we sing or how we pray. We can perform no vocational activity but what He is interested. One popular writer notes:

In recent generations, we have frequently limited the notion of a call to what is termed a "call to the ministry," meaning by this, in essence, a call to the pastorate or to a foreign mission field. The use of the term was not wrong, but it is woefully inadequate. Now we are finding . . . a conscious effort to recover the earlier and more vital conception. Today . . . young people pledge themselves to the ministry of farming and the ministry of medicine or law right along with those that pledge themselves to the ministry of the pastorate.[17]

C. *Freedom from Guilt*

Once after I had spoken about the doctrine of vocation, a physician said to me, "You cannot imagine how much guilt has been lifted from my shoulders by hearing this. I somehow thought that by going into a vocation other than pastoral ministry, I was something of a second-class citizen. I didn't realize the importance of my profession to God." An attorney spoke about the pressure he had felt as a young person when he told people he wanted to practice law. He was made to feel that this was a step down from the calling of pastoral ministry. For many years he experienced guilt as a result of this. Another person declared, "I have never heard anything like this before; this is so liberating. I am glad to know that my vocation is of importance to God."

Thomas Gillespie wrote:

> Each member of the *laos* stands under God's call and each is accountable for his or her response to it. In no way is this negated or compromised by the manner in which Paul speaks of himself as "called to be an apostle" (Romans 1:1; I Corinthians 1:1; cf. Galatians 1:1). The call of God is indeed individualized and particularized in concrete tasks, and Paul's apostleship is a prime example of this. But it may not be used to justify the view stemming from medieval times that only the "clergy" have a "calling" from God.[18]

Rather than saying, "I'm not a minister; I'm a carpenter," one should explain, "I'm a minister through my carpentry." To be a carpenter does not exclude one from ministerial standing.

There is a difference between *vocation* and *occupation*. Vocation is the call to be a servant of God in whatever work or occupation one is engaged. Occupation is the specific trade or profession in which one works. In other words, it is quite possible for one's occupation to change. But in the midst of that, the vocational calling is not altered. Vocation is a call to ministry regardless of what one's occupation may be. Vocational ministry, then, is not static but dynamic. Our sphere of ministry changes when we change occupationally, but our vocational calling remains crystal clear.

It was noted in one church conference that "the real battles of faith today are being fought in factories, shops, offices, and farms. In political parties and government agencies, in countless homes, in the press, on radio and television, in the relationship of nations. Very often it is said, that the church should 'go into these spheres' but the fact is that the church *is* already in these spheres in the persons of its laity."[19] When Paul wrote, "Whatever you do, do it all for the glory of God" (1 Cor. 10:31), he was not referring merely to pastors or to religious activities; he was referring to every activity in which the layperson is involved.

In looking at the four words "church," "ministry," "laity," and "vocation," we have a least briefly covered the major terms that help us begin to understand what it means to have a theology of the ministry of the laity.

Discussion Questions

1. Why is it important to have a theology of lay ministry?

2. How would you differentiate between a theology *for* laypersons and a theology *of* the laity?

3. What is meant by "incarnational theology"?

4. React to this statement: "The ministry of God's people is as much in the world as it is in the church."

5. How would you differentiate between the ministry of all believers and the specialized ministry of the clergy?

6. What is meant by the "theology of the dust mop"?

7. What is the difference between one's vocational ministry and one's occupation?

3

What History Tells Us

The concept of the ministry of the laity is not new. A brief look at the history of lay ministry can help us avoid some pitfalls and profit from prior successes. Whether we are laypersons or pastors, such a study can make us more effective in our ministry. If originally and biblically all Christians were considered ministers, how did we come to perceive of a few of God's people as ministers and of the rest of us as laity?

I. THE CLERGY-LAITY DICHOTOMY

A. *"Kleros" and "Laos"*

How did laity and clergy come to be seen as being so separate? One way to understand this is by looking at two Greek terms, *laos* and *kleros*. At first glance one might assume that *laos* means "laity" and *kleros* means "clergy." But we already know that *laos* means people—people of God. What does *kleros* mean? Does it refer to a separate group of people, an ordained group, comparable to our clergy? Not at all. *Kleros* simply means a "lot," or a "portion" of something—"a part," a selected part, a separate part. One might tend to think then that when the Greek word *kleros* appears in the New Testament, it refers to a select or separate group of people known as clergy. Strangely enough, such is not the case. For every time these two words, *kleros* and *laos*, appear they apply to the same people—to that portion of all humanity that walks with God.

51

As a follower of Christ you can say, "I am a part of the *laos* (the people of God), and I'm a part of the *kleros* (those especially set aside for service to God)." The separateness of clergy and laity was unknown in biblical times.

Elton Trueblood wrote:

> The contrast between the church at Corinth in the year 52 and the first congregational church of Technopolis in 1952 is really enormous. Owning no building, the Corinthian Christians made use of a synagogue or a private home . . . the picture which comes to us with such power is that of a fallible, yet devoted group, all of whom are on fire with missionary zeal and all of whom are engaged in the active ministry. All were of the laity in the sense that all were non-professional, but all were ministers in the sense that all ministered.[1]

While the term *laos* appears in the New Testament numerous times, the word *laikos*, which means "uneducated masses," appears nowhere in the New Testament. Strangely enough, today we have come to think of the laity as *laikos*—uneducated, untrained, non-seminary-educated persons.

The first use of the word "layperson" in Christian writings in this sense was in a letter written by Clement of Rome to the church in Corinth about A.D. 95 (1 Clement 40:6). In that letter, he contrasted the masses of people with the priests or Levites. Unfortunately, this distinction has continued through the centuries, and the dichotomy between clergy as the trained and laity as the untrained has remained.

Some of the church fathers in the early centuries of Christianity affirmed the ministry of the laity. Justin Martyr (ca. 100-165) and Irenaeus (ca. 115-200) properly portrayed the layperson as truly being a priest. Tertullian (ca. 160-230) noted that baptism could be regarded as the ordination of the laity. In contrast to these statements, a gradual separation developed between clergy and laity. As early as the writings of Jerome (ca. 340-420), clergy were regarded with a sense of the elite. Even the gradual development of the meaning of the word *kleros* demonstrates this fact. As Hans Küng noted,

> In Acts 1:26, the word *kleros* is used in its original sense, meaning that *lot* used as an expression of the will of God to determine who would be successor of Judas. From this original sense, the word *kleros* took on a more general sense of a

share which is allotted to someone . . . this led to the use of the word *"clerus"* . . . finally to refer to our holders of ecclesiastical office. As early as Origen (ca. 185-254), the word *kleros* has become an established term for those who hold office in the church, as opposed to the people. *"Clerus,"* for Jerome, are . . . the special property of the Lord or the Lord is their *lot,* their share."[2]

KLEROS

from:

"*lot*" or "*portions*" (all God's people)

to:

"*the Lord's portion*" (clergy only)

B. *From Function to Status*

While *kleros* originally applied to *all* God's people, the word early came to be used for a small, select group of people, separate from the rest of the *laos*. Then it developed, through the course of church history, into a group of persons elevated to special privilege. *Kleros* became equated with status.

All through church history we find that the body of people who came to be known as clergy became further and further separated from laypersons. The clergy was "accorded an increasingly privileged position and grew into a new sociological class of its own, with its own privileges, immunities, dress, titles, duties, and its own Latin culture, and its own Latin liturgy . . . In the early church there were differences of spiritual gifts and of tasks to fulfill, but there was no distinction between a group called clergy and a group called laity."[3]

Certainly we should all agree that the clergy have functions different from most laypersons for practical reasons. Not everyone, for example, needs to be standing and preaching on Sunday morning. That would be impractical. It would also be noisy! The distinction between clergy and laity should merely have been based on their different functions of ministry. There should never have been a separation based on the mistaken belief that some are ministers (clergy) and some are *not* ministers (laity).

We can look at the difference between clergy and laity one

other way. There is a legitimate distinction between clergy and laity today, but it is functional; it is based upon *what one does*. It is not ontological, that is, based upon *what one is* or one's essence.

Let me illustrate this distinction. I grew up on a farm where my dad taught us always to carry pliers. Now suppose I have a pair of pliers and a wrench in my hand. Is the difference between the pliers and the wrench functional or ontological? Are they different by what they do (functional) or by what they are (ontological)? The word "functional" is right. Pliers and a wrench certainly do different things; they are not used for exactly the same purposes. But they are ontologically the same (assuming they consist of identical metals). If I were to melt them down, I would find them blended into one. But if I were to take a pair of pliers and a banana, then what would we say? Are they functionally different? They surely are! And are they ontologically different? Yes! For a pair of pliers and a banana are different not only by what they *do* but also by what they *are*. Their very essence is completely different.

The difference between clergy and laity is a *legitimate difference*, but it is a difference *based upon function, not essence*. Any perception of clergy and laity that separates them by status is a misunderstanding of the universal call to ministry of *all* who are the people of God.

A clergyman or minister should not be raised on a pedestal, separated from others by status. A person working as a carpenter is doing something *functionally* different from a person who is preaching. No one questions that they are doing different things, but their separation is purely by what they *do*, not by what they *are*. *Both* are called to ministry. They are simply called to *different* ministries.

C. *The Gap Grows*

As we continue our walk through Church history, the gulf between clergy and laity widens. By the end of the second century, laity, for the most part, were seldom allowed to teach in the church. As early as A.D. 325, in the Council of Nicea, the church was defined as the "Clerical Order." The church by definition consisted of the clergy. Thus the phrase developed "The church is where the bishop is." The bishop was the overseer of the congregation. Tragically, that definition of the church left out most of the persons who comprised the church.

As early as the year 250, ordination became a permanent step in the church. It was often misused to separate clergy and laity. Certainly ordination is important and valid today. However, it is not valid to use it to make laypersons feel they are not ministers.

This is not to suggest that the early leaders of the Christian Church were power-hungry deviants who attempted to rob laypersons of their ministries. Far from it. Many external pres-

PRESSURES: 1. _Wrong Teaching_

2. _Paganism_

3. _Persecution_

RESULTS: 1. _Creeds_

2. _Canon (Bible)_

3. _Clergy_

sures on the early Christian leaders seemed to push them in these directions. For example, a great amount of wrong teaching circulated among the early Christians. Such movements as Gnosticism and Montanism threatened the purity of the faith. Paganism and persecution were also constant threats to the Early Church. These kinds of pressures prompted three developments: (1) the development of creeds so the people would know what they believed and what not to believe; (2) the development of the canon of the Scriptures so the Church would have an authority to which it could turn; (3) the development of the clergy so certain persons would be specifically trained to defend and sustain the faith.

By the fourth century, the *Apostolic Constitutions* stated that the laity should merely "sit and amen." That is not unlike our contemporary treatment of laypersons—what some have called the "pay, pray, and obey syndrome."

Perhaps no period of church history more clearly reveals the separation between clergy and laity than the medieval years, the millennium between A.D. 590 and 1517. Two enormous barriers separated clergy and laity even further. One was the language barrier. The worship service was spoken in a language the attenders could not even understand. The second barrier was the sacramental barrier. It was taught as a doctrine that one must receive the sacraments on a regular basis to be assured of the kingdom of heaven. This meant that the village priest, by merely refusing the sacraments to a layperson, could prevent that person from entering heaven. In the palm of the hand the clergy held either eternal reward or damnation for the layperson. Some historians argue that this sacramental theology was one of the major causes of the widening gulf between clergy and laity.

Christopher Brooke noted, "There was no more fundamental division in medieval life than the division between clergy and laity."[4] Perhaps one of the most interesting church declarations ever made was made in the Council of Seville in A.D. 619, when it was decided that laity should remain separate from the clergy. The scriptural justification for such a ruling was based upon Deut. 22:10, which states that an ox and a donkey should not plow together. A quotation from Ignatius reveals the fear some laypersons had of their clergy: "He that honors the bishop, shall

"Ministry" and Laity Separated

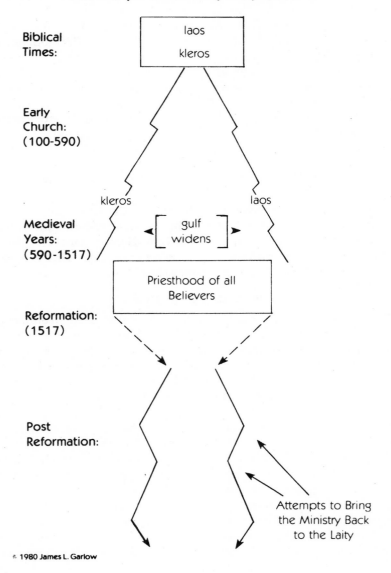

Biblical
Times:

laos

kleros

Early
Church:
(100-590)

Medieval
Years:
(590-1517)

kleros

laos

gulf
widens

Priesthood of all
Believers

Reformation:
(1517)

Post
Reformation:

Attempts to Bring
the Ministry Back
to the Laity

© 1980 James L. Garlow

be honored by God; he that does anything without the knowledge of the bishop serves the Devil."[5]

During the Middle Ages there were only two major lay activities. One was the Crusades, a series of attempts by Christians to capture portions of the Holy Land. It is tragic that the Church, which claimed to be founded by the Prince of Peace, seemed during this period to bring out the most warlike tendencies in its people. During these years Christianity was never able to properly direct the enthusiasm of its laity. The other lay activity was the building of cathedrals. Though this is not often seen as a lay ministry, the artisans and craftsmen of the day appropriately considered these activities expressions of praise to God.

II. LAY PREACHING MOVEMENTS

Throughout much of the history of the Christian Church, there have been attempts by the laity to proclaim the Good News. Some of these movements were clearly heretical. Others were led by well-meaning, well-intentioned laypersons who felt that the established clergy were not doing the job.

A. *Medieval Attempts and Opposition*

Church leaders reacted and responded to these movements in varying ways. In the year 692, the Trullan Council decreed that laypersons should not be allowed to preach any longer in public services. Pope Leo I issued a ban on lay preaching at two different church councils—one at Tours in 813 and one at Aachen in 836. These bans reveal that lay preaching was certainly occurring.

Two well-known figures of church history, Dominic (1170-1221) and Francis (1182-1226), founded preaching orders that originally had lay status. Dominic's preachers were an elite corps of missionaries who lived lives of total poverty and self-denial. Francis's preachers, originally known as the preachers of penance, were concerned for the poor. Other lay preaching movements were led by such figures as Peter of Bruys and Henry Monk. Another little-known lay preaching movement of the 11th century was the Milanese Patarines. Slightly better known is an interesting movement known as the Waldenses, guided by

Peter Waldo (1140-87). Waldo's lay preachers were known as the Poor Men of Lyons. This group soon became very anticlerical. They experienced much conflict with church leaders. In contrast to this, the Franciscans (the followers of Francis) were not anticlerical and chose to work with ecclesiastical support.

Two popes, Alexander III (?-1181) and Lucius III (1097-1185), attempted to halt lay preaching. In contrast to them, Pope Innocent III (1160-1216) provided opportunity for lay preaching. One group of laypersons that Pope Innocent allowed to preach was known as the Humiliati from northern Italy. By 1215, the Fourth Lateran Synod, a church council, banned lay preaching for the whole Catholic church.

One of the better-known trainers of lay preachers was John Wycliffe (ca. 1320-84). He and his English poor preachers condemned the corruption of the church. Wycliffe rejected the separation of clergy and laity. He founded hundreds of small-group home Bible studies. The Council of Trent, a Catholic church council held from 1545 to 1563, decided that sermons should be preached only by bishops and the clergy. This restriction on lay preaching found its way into the *Codex Juris Canonicis* of 1917, effective the next year. Ironically, a layman by the name of Lodovico Nogorola preached at the Council of Trent, the very council that outlawed lay preaching!

B. *English Efforts*

Lay preaching flourished during the 1500s and 1600s in England. Robert Brown and Henry Barrowe were two Englishmen who advocated that all persons should be allowed to preach. John Taylor, in the mid-1600s, argued against laity who would leave their vocational pursuits in order to preach. Thomas Hall and Thomas Collier, writing in England in 1651, argued regarding lay preaching. Hall claimed that laity were ignorant and should not preach. Collier claimed that the apostles themselves were unlearned men. Since the apostles preached, so could any layperson, said Collier. Englishman Don Lupton defended lay preaching in a 1651 tract on the grounds that hiding one's talents was a sin before God. John Martin joined the controversy in a tract titled *The Preacher Sent*. While he admitted that lay preaching had suffered many abuses, he stated, "The abuse of a good thing does not invalidate the thing itself."

The lay preaching fury that occurred in England in the 1500s and 1600s declined noticeably from 1660 throughout the first third of the 1700s. It is interesting to observe the intense desire of so many laypersons to be involved in ministry. Certainly there are numerous ministries besides preaching. However, it was lay preaching that seemed to capture the hearts of so many of God's people during the medieval years.

It should be noted that lay preaching is being encouraged by church leadership. Some denominations are providing thorough training for those who choose to remain laity yet desire to be involved in the ministry of preaching. Hans Küng noted that

> there would seem to be very good reasons for a revival of the idea of lay preaching, provided it suited existing conditions and was properly ordered; this view is supported not only by the New Testament, but by the present situation both in the world—particularly the diminished power of the Church and the development of the secular world—and in the Church—particularly the lack of preachers and the maturity of the laity. . . . This does not of course mean that every Christian, while as a Christian he is called to preach the word and to give personal witness to his faith, is necessarily called to give sermons in the community. The charisms of the Spirit are various. On the other hand, charisms which have been granted to Christians ought to be acknowledged with gratitude and pressed into service. In this way sermons by lay people will be possible without specific ecclesiastical permission or training.[6]

C. *Luther Leads the Reformers*

The separation between the clergy and the laity appears to widen throughout much of church history. The clergy became *the* ministers; laity to a large extent assumed a passive role. Of the many attempts to correct this imbalance, the best known is the Protestant Reformation. In the year 1517, Martin Luther did a very usual thing that brought unusual results. He listed several issues for public debate and posted them on the church door. This was a common practice in Martin Luther's time. What Martin Luther had not counted on was someone's taking these 95 grievances or theses, as they were called, printing them up, and spreading them all over Germany.

From those statements Luther posted on the door that day came a movement—a movement that reached beyond Germany to many other countries as well. It was a time of tremendous theological, political, and social upheaval. The theology of Martin Luther is often summarized in what is called the Four *Solas: Sola Fide, Sola Christa, Sola Gratia,* and *Sola Scriptura*—"Faith alone, Christ alone, grace alone, and Scripture alone."

Reformation theology brought profound implications. It impacted many aspects of life in Germany. One issue to which Luther spoke directly was the ministry of the laity. In 1520, he wrote three treatises—one of which is titled *To the German Nobility.* In that treatise he made this controversial announcement, "There is . . . really no difference between laypersons, priests, princes, bishops, or in Romanist terminology, between religious and secular, than that of office or occupation, and not that of Christian status. All have spiritual status, and all are truly priests, bishops, and popes." What was Luther saying? He was saying that laypersons should view themselves as being truly ministers and priests. That does not sound so new to us now. But if we had been living in 16th-century Germany, that would have been explosive language.

Probably the most popular phrase that came out of the Reformation was "the priesthood of all believers." It is also likely the most misunderstood phrase of the Reformation. It does not mean that every person is his or her *own* priest. It does mean that everyone functions as a priest *to others.* I do not priest myself. I am not somehow able to function in isolation from other Christians. Rather, we stand as priests before God *to other Christians.* Furthermore, the priesthood that is spoken of in the phrase "priesthood of all believers" is not based upon *privilege* but upon *service.* I can never pat myself on the back and say, "My, am I not impressive! I am a priest!" No, my priesthood is a call to *servanthood.*

It should not have surprised people in Luther's day (and it should not surprise us) that we all have a priesthood. Even a casual glance at 1 Peter, chapter 2, tells us that all believers are priests. The Book of Hebrews tells us that all Christians are priests and are to offer sacrifices. One does not become a priest by being ordained. A person becomes a priest by joining the community of faith, by becoming part of the people of God. The New Testament speaks of only two priesthoods—*first,* that of Christ; and *second,* that of all believers.

The Reformation highlighted not only the churchly ministries of laypersons but also their vocational ministries. In Christian theology, *vocation* generally has two meanings. First, it can mean a call to repentance and faith. But for our purposes we are more concerned with a second definition, and that is the call to serve one's neighbor in the world. Luther made no distinction between the sacred (the spiritual) and the profane (the secular). He understood that God saw no separation. To Luther, the act of farming or functioning as a milkmaid was every bit as important in God's sight as that of preaching. For Luther, the ministry of the laity clearly included one's relationship to brothers and sisters.

The person who belonged to Christ

> fulfilled the command to love his neighbor through the roles or callings or stations he had in life. These stations (for example: husband, wife, businessman, milkmaid, etc.) were concrete embodiments of the natural law, and to neglect these responsibilities was to disobey the will of God. The impact of Luther's view was (1) to deprive churchly or religious vocations of any special merit, and, in fact, to criticize them as irresponsible if they seduced one away from one's concrete, daily duties, and (2) to interpret all useful secular vocations as having a positive religious meaning.[7]

Probably one of the most profound statements on the vocational ministry of the laity, from about the same time period, was made by William Tyndale (1494-1536). He wrote:

> Thou that ministerest in the kitchen, and art but a kitchen page . . . knowest that God hath put thee in that office . . . if thou compared deed and deed, there is a difference between washing of dishes and preaching of the Word of God; but as touching to please God, none at all . . . let every man, whether . . . tailor . . . merchant or husband refer his craft and occupation under the common wealth and serve his brethren as he would to Christ Himself.[8]

No one single movement more self-consciously reclaimed a theology of lay ministry than did the Reformation. In a sense, it is kind of a watershed. Many spokespeople today for the priesthood of all believers point back to the Reformation as a movement that has never been completed. It is in that sense that the Reformation is important.

Numerous post-Reformation movements attempted to reclaim ministry for laypersons. Philipp Spener (1635-1705), a German pastor, was persuaded that the priesthood of all believers needed to be put into actual practice. He made many creative attempts. Nikilaus von Zinzendorf (1700-69), the German leader of the Moravians, used laypersons extensively for ministry. One of the persons who studied Zinzendorf's use of the laity was an Englishman named John Wesley, who used laypersons in many ways.

III. JOHN WESLEY'S USE OF THE LAITY

A. *His Greatest Work*

What do you think of when you hear the name John Wesley? For many of us, he has been associated so closely with the doctrine of Christian perfection that we tend to think of nothing but that. Wesley, of course, said and did many other creative things. His most outstanding contribution to Christianity was probably not in the things we commonly associate with Wesley. Rather, it was his extensive training and utilization of the laity for meaningful, systematic, and consistent ministry.

One would be hard-pressed to find a more outstanding example of lay ministry training than John Wesley. British Methodism would not have existed without its extensive utilization of the laity. From its beginning, it was primarily a lay movement. Its uniqueness was not so much in the fact that it used the laity, but in the *extent* to which they were used. Franz Hildebrandt suggested that "the scale on which Wesley recruited these forces in the service of Methodism was something of a revolution in Church history."[9] Anglican Bishop Stephen Neill made a similar point regarding Wesley's class leaders, noting that it was a "calling of the layman into responsible activity in the church on a scale that had hardly ever been before."[10]

One way to measure the extent of Wesley's reliance on laypersons is to measure the amount of criticism directed at him for his lay ministry practices. Wesley was criticized for many things, but mostly for two practices: (1) field preaching, and (2) the use of laypersons as preachers. He was criticized by his Anglican colleagues. Even his brother Charles cautioned him strongly that allowing laypersons to be so involved in ministry was a dangerous innovation.

Wesley trained 653 lay preachers during his half century of active ministry. Between 1739 and 1765, he trained 193 lay preachers. From 1765 to 1790, he trained 460 lay preachers. It is interesting to observe that 40 percent of those in the earlier group stayed with him in ministry until their deaths, whereas in the second group 65 percent of those continued to work with Wesley until they died (or until he died). Of the 653 that he trained, 374 (57 percent) continued to work with him throughout their life spans. In other words, his attrition rate was reduced over the years. He became more effective in the selectivity and training of laypersons.

YEARS	LAY PASTORS	%
1739-1765	193	40
1765-1790	460	65
TOTAL	653	57

It is not certain when Wesley first utilized the layperson to preach. Some think that the first lay preacher's name was Humphreys. Others feel that it may have been John Cennick. Tradition has it that it was Thomas Maxfield. According to this account, John Wesley failed to arrive in London in time for one of his preaching engagements. It so happened that a layperson by the name of Thomas Maxfield was presiding in that service. After waiting at length for Wesley to arrive, Maxfield finally stepped to the pulpit and began to preach. When Wesley returned to London and learned about this, he was furious. On his way to rebuke Maxfield, John Wesley's mother, Susanna, strongly admonished him to reconsider. She reminded him that Thomas Maxfield was as called to minister as John Wesley was. Wesley considered her words seriously and began to use laity as lay preachers.

Within a relatively short period of time, an army of laypersons had been raised up to impact England. Wesley did not do this because he had a theology of the ministry of the laity. Wesley was an innovator. He wanted to communicate the gospel to the masses. He could accomplish this with laypersons. Wesley's actions often came first; his theology was ordinarily hammered out later. Wesley initially utilized laity by default, not by design.

The major difference between Wesley's lay preachers and some of the other lay preaching movements that preceded it is in its relationship to clergy. Some of the lay preaching movements of the Middle Ages were anticlerical. Some of them viciously attacked the established church. Wesley attempted to avoid this. He understood that laity, if they were to be trained properly, needed enablers.

Those best qualified to equip laypersons for their ministry are usually clergy. Wesley relied heavily on a small group of clergy to assist him in training laypersons for their ministries. They assisted him in motivating, training, and equipping the vast army of laypersons that were sent across England and later to America. He actively recruited Anglican priests for this task. Unfortunately, few responded. Probably no more than 40 Anglican priests were truly sympathetic to Wesley. However, several Anglican priests were invaluable to Wesley in assisting his army of laypersons.

Wesley organized these lay preachers into traveling circuits, organized tours. In 1746, there were only six such organized tours. By the time of Wesley's death in 1791, lay preachers were presenting the gospel to the teeming masses of England on over 114 circuits.

B. *Duties of a Lay Preacher*

What did a lay preacher do? Obviously, preached. Wesley wrote extensive guidelines for his lay preachers on what to preach, how to preach, to whom to preach, and where to preach. What to preach? Christ. Wesley's lay preachers were forbidden to preach on "notions"—in other words, their own pet peeves. He even wrote a list of these notions so that no lay preacher would accidentally start speaking on things other than Christ. It was most important to Wesley that his lay preachers talk about the redemptive love of Christ.

How to preach? Preach simply, in a manner that even the most common person could understand the essence of the gospel. He wanted his people to speak plain truths for plain people in plain words. To whom should they preach? To everyone who would listen, but primarily to the poor. Wesley was quite concerned that the gospel be presented to those who had little of this world's earthly goods. Where should they preach? Anywhere, even if it was outdoors. In fact, Wesley was strongly criticized for a practice known as field preaching. But he was convinced that his lay preachers had not used field preaching enough. He urged, "We cannot expect people to come to us. We must go and seek them. We must use it more."

Not only did Wesley's lay preachers preach but they also pastored. The lay preachers provided primary pastoral shepherding care for thousands of England's young converts. One scholar noted that not since the apostolic age had one ever exercised so much immediate pastoral care as Wesley did. He trained his lay preachers to give the same kind of careful oversight.

Wesley's lay preachers did more than just preach and pastor. They did a lot of singing, for singing was very important to the Methodist revival. Although John and Charles Wesley wrote many of the hymns that were sung, Wesley urged his lay preachers to refrain from songwriting. It seems that some had tried. Those particular songs had poor meter and were almost impossible to sing. In contrast to this, he did encourage them to write their memoirs. He did not hesitate to publish these as well. As a result, one can read extensive notes from the lives of many of the lay preachers. It was important, Wesley felt, to keep a careful journal of one's spiritual pilgrimage.

C. *Other Leadership*

Lay preachers were not the only laypersons Wesley trained. For a time he had a group known as local preachers. In addition, he had class leaders who had spiritual oversight over a group of about a dozen people. The class leader monitored the spiritual progress of each person in his or her group. Besides classes, there were bands. The bands were smaller, generally four or five people, and consisted of persons of the same sex and marital status. They would gather for more intimate sharing of their Christian walk.

Then Wesley had exhorters. The exhorter would speak before the group to admonish, warn, or encourage. In contrast to a lay preacher, an exhorter was not supposed to take a text. He or she could not take a passage from the Scripture and elaborate on it. Only a lay preacher could do that. In addition to these lay ministry positions, Wesley had trustees and stewards. He also created a category known as the visitors of the sick. John Wesley probably had the most extensive network of laypersons trained for ministry ever known in the history of Christianity. Little we could do or say today would improve upon what he did in this area some 200 years ago.[11]

One of Wesley's lay preachers, Francis Asbury, was sent to America in 1771 at the age of 26. He later became the first bishop of American Methodism. The major reason Methodism spread across this country at such an unparalleled pace was Asbury's extensive deployment of lay preachers. Methodism was not the only denomination to grow rapidly in America. The Baptist faith also spread quickly across the wilderness and the prairies. That was likewise due to the extensive use of laity. Alexander Campbell founded a group now known as the Disciples of Christ. Their rapid growth in 19th-century America can be attributed almost entirely to their emphasis upon the ministry of all of God's people.

Those who lived in the centuries before us have much to contribute to present-day thinking about the role of laypersons in ministry. Pastors and laypersons alike can reap great dividends by exploring the ministry of the laity in the movements that have gone before us. We are a part of a long, rich heritage—a heritage that repeatedly affirms that all God's people are ministers.

DISCUSSION QUESTIONS

1. What is your reaction to the following statement? "The difference between clergy and laity is a legitimate difference, but it is a difference based upon function and not essence."

2. What is meant by the expression "the priesthood of believers"?

3. What did Martin Luther mean by vocational ministries?

4. Why did some of the early lay preaching movements fail?

5. How extensive was John Wesley's use of lay preachers?

6. How much use did John Wesley make of the small-group technique?

4

Our Gifts for Ministry

Christians today show a renewed interest in the gifts of the Spirit. This is a healthy trend. God has given us special gifts by which we can better serve Him and our fellow human beings.

This strong interest in gifts has its dangers, however. It is possible to slip into the error of gift obsession. This occurs when followers of Christ forget that gifts are means to an end, not ends in themselves. God gives gifts for service or ministry. Our fascination should not be with our gifts but rather with the God who gives them and in whose service those gifts will be employed.

Unfortunately, many people know neither what their gifts are nor how to discover those gifts. According to James Engel and H. Wilbert Norton, "Surveys are now beginning to disclose that most Christians either do not know their spiritual gift or do not know how to exercise it within the body. Therefore, a fundamental ministry of cultivation of the believers is to uncover these gifts and train the believer to their use."[1]

I. Agape Love

As we begin our study of the gifts of the Spirit, we need to heed the warning of the apostle Paul. He reminds us that love—*agape* love—is more important than seeking one's gift. Above all else, *agape* should characterize our ministry. *Agape*, more than anything else, should be expressed in our actions.

The Greek language has more than one word for love. *Phileo*

LOVE:

1. _Phileo_
2. _eros_
3. _Storge_
4. Agape

love is a brotherly love. "Philadelphia" means "city of brotherly love." A third kind of love is *eros* love, sensual love. It is sometimes sexual, though not always. *Eros* love is attracted to another for what it can get back from him or her. A fourth kind of love is *storge* love, a love between blood relatives. This word is not used in the New Testament. The kind of love we are concerned with here is agape love. If it is as important as Paul says, we ought to examine its characteristics.

What are the characteristics of agape? First of all, *agape is spontaneous.*[2] It is a kind of love that would cause a perfect God to love a sinner. If God loved only the righteous, we would all be left out. It is different from the kind of love we express so often as humans. We tend to respond most positively to those who respond positively to us. Agape love is different. It is not motivated by what it sees in the one receiving that love. It is spontaneous.

Second, agape love is *indifferent to value.* There is no particular scale of worth by which agape love measures those who are to receive love. Such things as education, wealth, prestige, social status, and beauty are unimportant to agape love. Acts 10:34 states, "God is no respecter of persons" (KJV). When we look through the lens of agape love at other persons, we do not see certain people as more important than others.

Third, agape love is *creative.* It creates value in those who receive it. Agape is a value-creating principle. Many today lack self-worth, self-esteem. If somehow persons could become aware that they are loved by God and by others, much emotional stress could be eliminated. Agape love creates a sense of worth.

Fourth, agape love is an *initiator of fellowship*. Humankind is not the creator of fellowship with God; rather, God is. His love reaches out to form a bridge. Religion, we are told, is a person striving to reach God; whereas Christianity is the story of God reaching to His people. That is agape love—God reaching out compassionately to His children. We enjoy a relationship with God because He first reached to us in love. As our ministry reflects this agape love, we will find ourselves reaching out to establish fellowship with others.

Fifth, agape love is *eternal*. According to 1 Cor. 13:8, it never ends.

Sixth, agape love is *comprehensive*. It fulfills the law. It not only obeys the law but also fulfills it—in all of its demands.

AGAPE

1. *Spontaneous*

Romans 5:5

2. *indifferent to Value*

Romans 5:8, Galatians 5:13

3. *Creative*

Galatians 5:13

4. *initiator of fellowship*

Romans 5:8

5. *eternal*

1 Corinthians 13:13

The agape love that should characterize each of our ministries is a love that is spontaneous, indifferent to value, creative, an initiator of fellowship, never-ending, and comprehensive.

Agape is "that something without which everything else is nothing." It "would be all-sufficient even if it were alone." It "is not merely an attribute of God, it is His very nature."[3]

II. Learning to Express Agape

We were created to express agape love, yet we cannot express it in our own natural, human strength. Agape love is expressed only by the power of Christ. Furthermore, expressing agape love is an exercise of the total personality. It involves the will. Paul commands, "Follow the way of love" (1 Cor. 14:1), or *pursue* love.

Paul give us another guideline: "Be imitators of God, therefore, as dearly loved children and live a life of love, just as Christ loved us and gave himself up for us as a fragrant offering and sacrifice to God" (Eph. 5:1-2). Paul is telling us to become *copyists* of God. The word "imitator" here is a strong term. This verse tells us to become more than followers. We are to become a divine copy, to imitate means to become like another. Paul says, "Live a life of love." Some translations read, "Walk in love." Walking implies a mode of life. It means to live in agape, to have constancy in lifestyle.

Paul gives us an additional guideline: "Therefore, as God's chosen people, holy and dearly loved, clothe yourselves with compassion, kindness, humility, gentleness and patience. Bear with each other and forgive whatever grievances you may have against one another. Forgive as the Lord forgave you. And over all these virtues put on love, which binds them all together in perfect unity" (Col. 3:12-14).

The clothes mentioned in verse 12 were like undercoats or undergarments. Persons hearing this verse in Bible times would have no problem understanding what Paul was saying. In the Eastern world, the outer garment was wrapped around tightly in such a way that it held all the undergarments together. This outer garment played a very important role. If the outer garment came loose, the rest of one's attire was in jeopardy. And our Christian lives are in jeopardy without agape love. Paul is implying, "If you lose agape, you have lost everything." Agape is that one quality that brings everything into the proper balance and proper relationship. So important was agape that Paul equates it to that crucial outer garment.

In Galatians, chapter 5, we have a list known as the fruit of the Spirit, containing individual characteristics of the Christian life. Some have assumed that since agape love is in this list it has no more importance than the other qualities mentioned—such as kindness and humility. Such is not the case. Agape is that one word that describes the sum total of all the other characteristics. Agape is not merely one in a list of things. It is the comprehensive result when all of the others are present.

Regardless of what gifts you have, the one single characterization of your ministry should be agape. Remember, after Paul completed his teaching on the gifts and before he began his discussion of agape, he wrote, "And now I will show you the most excellent way" (1 Cor. 12:31). That way is the way of love.

III. WHAT ARE THE GIFTS?

God has given us gifts so that we can respond to His call to ministry. Ray Stedman stated, "To become aware that God, Himself, has equipped you—YES, YOU—with a uniquely designed pattern of spiritual gifts and has placed you exactly where He wants you in order to minister those gifts, is to enter a whole new dimension of exciting possibilities. In all the world, there is no experience more satisfying and fulfilling than to realize that you have been the instrument of the divine working in the lives of others."[4]

	TALENT	GIFTS
Source:	Common grace of Spirit	Special grace of Spirit
Time Given:	Present from natural birth	Present from new birth
Nature:	Natural ability	Spiritual endowment
Purpose:	Instruction, entertainment, inspiration on a natural level	Spiritual growth of saints, Christian service

In our discussion of gifts, it might be helpful to distinguish between talents and gifts. Leslie B. Flynn makes the distinction in this way:

> Whereas talents are a common gift given to all persons, gifts are a special grace or gift given to those who are believers. A talent is present from natural birth, in contrast to a gift, which is present from the new birth. A talent may be understood as a natural ability, in contrast a gift is a spiritual endowment. A talent can be used for instruction or entertainment or inspiration on a natural level. A gift, however, has a distinctly spiritual purpose. It is for the growth of believers and for the encouragement of persons in Christian service.[5]

Spiritual gifts are mentioned primarily in three New Testament letters: Rom. 12:6-8; 1 Cor. 12:4-11, 28; and Eph. 4:11.

To the Romans Paul wrote:

1. Rom. 12:6-8

    We have different gifts, according to the grace given us. If a man's gift is prophesying, let him use it in proportion to his faith. If it is serving, let him serve; if it is teaching, let him teach; if it is encouraging, let him encourage; if it is contributing to the needs of others, let him give generously; if it is leadership, let him govern diligently; if it is showing mercy, let him do it cheerfully.

GIFTS 1) prophecy   5) giving
2) serving   6) Leadership
3) teaching   7) Mercy
4) Exhortation (encouraging)

The gifts listed here are prophecy, serving, teaching, exhortation (encouraging), giving, leadership, and mercy.

To the Corinthians Paul wrote:

2. 1 Cor. 12:4-11

    There are different kinds of gifts, but the same Spirit. There are different kinds of service, but the same Lord. There are different kinds of working, but the same God works all of them in all men.

    Now to each one the manifestation of the Spirit is given for the common good. To one there is given through the Spirit the message of wisdom, to another the message of knowledge by means of the same

Spirit, to another faith by the same Spirit, to another gifts of healing by that one Spirit, to another miraculous powers, to another prophecy, to another distinguishing between spirits, to another speaking in different kinds of tongues, and to still another the interpretation of tongues. All these are the work of one and the same Spirit, and he gives them to each one, just as he determines.

GIFTS
1) wisdom
2) knowledge
3) faith
4) healing
5) work miracles
6) prophecy
7) discernment of spirits
8) tongues
9) interpretation of tongues

The gifts listed here are wisdom, knowledge, faith, healing, working miracles, prophecy, discernment, tongues, and interpretation of tongues. Paul also wrote:

3. 1 Cor. 12:28

And in the church God has appointed first of all apostles, second prophets, third teachers, then workers of miracles, also those having gifts of healing, those able to help others, those with gifts of administration, and those speaking in different kinds of tongues.

GIFTS
1) apostleship
2) prophecy
3) teaching
4) working miracles
5) healing
6) helps
7) administration
8) tongues

The gifts spoken of here are apostleship, prophecy, teaching, working miracles, healing, helps, administration, and tongues.

To the Ephesians Paul wrote:

4. Eph. 4:11

It was he who gave some to be apostles, some to be prophets, some to be evangelists, and some to be pastors and teachers.

GIFTS *1 apostles*
2 prophets
3 evangelists
4 pastor / teachers

    The gifts referred to here are apostles, prophets, evangelists, pastors, and teachers. Frequently the last gift is referred to as a hyphenated gift, pastor-teacher. One useful way of listing the gifts would be in the following manner:

Kenneth Kinghorn ("Gifts of the Spirit," p. 38) listed the gifts in the following manner:			
Rom. 12:6-8	1 Cor. 12:4-11	1 Cor. 12:28	Eph. 4:11
Prophecy Teaching Serving Exhortation Giving Giving Aid Compassion	Prophecy	Prophecy Teaching	Prophecy Teaching
	Healing Working miracles Tongues Interpretation of tongues Wisdom Knowledge Faith Discernment	Healing Working miracles Tongues Interpretation of tongues	
		Apostleship Helps Administration	Apostleship
			Evangelism Shepherding

Another useful gift list is provided to us by Ray Hurn in his leader's guide titled *Strategy Manual for Finding Your Ministry*. He lists the gifts as follows:

Eph. 4	apostles
	prophets
	evangelists
	pastors
	teachers
Rom. 12	prophesying
	servings
	teaching
	exhortation
	giving
	leading
	showing mercy
1 Cor. 12	wisdom
	knowledge
	faith
	healing
	miracles
	prophecy
	distinguishing of spirits
	tongues (languages)
	interpretation of tongues (languages)[6]

How many gifts are there? It is difficult to say. Some writers state that there are only 19. Others have another definite number. Some writers do not think Paul's list is necessarily comprehensive. It is not immediately apparent that Paul intended to name every single gift. Nevertheless, his gift lists are sufficiently complete to assist us in finding a ministry.

IV. DANGERS CONCERNING GIFTS

There are some dangers related to the study of spiritual gifts. One of these occurs when a person assumes that since he or she possesses a certain gift, everyone else should have the same one. This is not uncommon with people who have gifts that are highly visible in the Christian Body. Another danger is that of becoming so obsessed with understanding our gifts that we ignore the basic steps toward Christian maturity. It is possible to focus my attention so much on my gifts that I give inadequate attention to a consistent day-by-day walk with Christ.

Another danger is when I assume that my gift is more important than your gift. First, the gifts are not mine and yours; they are His. He gave them to us. Second, we should not assume that just because some gifts are more obvious to the Christian Body this automatically makes them more important. This often occurs with the gift of evangelism. Those who have the gift of evangelism generally have a high visibility in the Christian body. There is a tendency to assume that the gift is more important than others. No one denies the importance of the gift of evangelism. The problem begins when we assume that it is *more* important than all the other gifts that God has chosen to give.

Another warning needs to be sounded regarding spiritual gifts. We should remember that they are truly *gifts*. That is, they were given to us by God. We did nothing to merit them, so we deserve no credit for having them. One of the worst things that could occur in studying gifts would be to discover our gifts, then fail to employ them in the service of the One who gave them to us. This would defeat the whole purpose for studying gifts. Gifts are given to be used in His service for His honor.

There is a distinction between gift and ministry. God gives you a specific gift that is exercised in a ministry. For example, hospitality is a gift. The way you use that gift is your ministry. You might use it to host a Bible study in your home. You might use it to provide short-term lodging to persons in need of shelter. Your home might become a center for coffee-cup gatherings for your neighborhood. Any of these could become your ministry, but your gift remains the same—hospitality. Your ministry, then, is simply the way or sphere in which you exercise your gift.

V. Discovering Our Spiritual Gifts

The apostle Paul makes an interesting statement in his first letter to the Corinthians: "There are varieties of working, but it is the same God who inspires them all in every one" (1 Cor. 12:6,

RSV). Notice the word "working." It is sometimes translated "energizing." According to Ray Stedman, this word refers to the

> degree of power by which a gift is manifested or ministered on a specific occasion . . . Every exercise of a spiritual gift does not produce the same result each time. The same message given in several different circumstances will not produce the same results. What is the difference? It is God's choice. He does not intend to produce the same results everytime. He could, but He does not always desire to do so. It is up to the Father to determine how much is accomplished at each ministry of a gift.[7]

Another writer gives a slightly different definition for the term "working" or "energizing." He prefers the word "results."[8] Kenneth Kinghorn gives the example of one who has the gift for teaching. That gift might be exercised in such ministries as preaching, writing, and counseling. Now each one of these three have different results—the working or energizing mentioned by Paul. The results of the ministry of preaching, for example, might be Christian conversion. The results of the ministry of writing could be Christian growth. The results of the ministry of counseling might be Christian unity. The gift is teaching, but there are at least three different ministries where that gift can be exercised. The results from those three ministries are all different—conversion, growth, and unity.

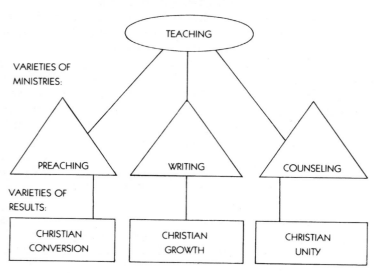

78

According to Dr. Kinghorn, the word "results" or "workings" refers to a *qualitative* difference. However, for Dr. Stedman the word "workings" refers to a *quantitative* difference—a difference in amount. In all probability both interpretations are correct. Certainly both differences occur in real life. The results of the exercise of our gifts in various ministries are often different. Our task is to faithfully utilize our gifts in a meaningful area of ministry. The results are in God's hands.

You will note that we have not defined the gifts of the Spirit. One reason for this omission is that much has already been written on the definitions of the gifts (see Appendix B). In addition, our major concern here is to know how to discover our spiritual gifts. Gift discovery is vitally important to lay ministry. One writer warned that, "The use of spiritual gifts diminishes when the role of the laity is reduced. . . . When the role of the clergy develops into performing the ministry described by the spiritual gifts, the use of those gifts diminishes; so does the part of the laity."[9]

How can you know your spiritual gifts? How do you go about discovering them? In his book *Gifts of the Spirit* (pp. 108-16), Dr. Kenneth Kinghorn suggests six steps to finding your gifts. I would like to expand on those six steps and diagram them for you. First, open yourself to God as a channel for His use. Second, examine your aspirations for Christian service in ministry. Third, identify the needs you believe to be most crucial in the life of the church. Fourth, evaluate the results of your efforts to serve and to minister. Fifth, follow the guidance of the Holy Spirit, as He leads you into obedience to Christ. Sixth, remain alert to the responses of other Christians.

In the diagram below are six numbers corresponding with the six statements above. In the circle that says "number one" let's write the word *you*. Open yourself to God as a channel for His use. The *first step* in finding your gifts is attitudinal. What is your attitude regarding being of service or ministry to Him? Do you really want to know where you fit in the kingdom of God? Do you desire to know what your gifts are and how they can be used to bring honor to Him? If your answer is yes, then you are ready to move on to step two.

Let's diagram those suggestions.

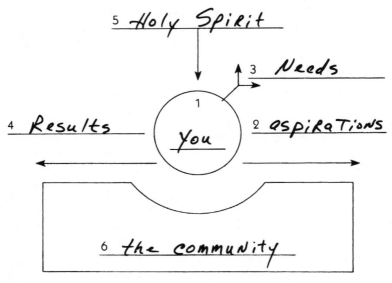

Step two can be summarized in one word—*aspirations*. What are your goals and your aspirations for ministry? If I were to sit down with you and ask you the question "What would you most like to accomplish for God?" you would probably list three or four things that you would like to see happen. Those aspirations might give me some clue as to your gifts. People's goals or aspirations generally are closely related to the gifts needed to reach these goals. The gifts required to meet your goals are likely gifts you actually have.

Let's look at a *third step*. The key word here is "needs." As you look around you in your local church fellowship and the larger Body of Christ, what needs do you think are most critical? In what areas does the Body of Christ seem to be lacking the most? Write down on a sheet of paper the greatest needs you see in your congregation. Once again, there is a strong possibility that the gifts required to meet those needs are gifts that you have. Why is that? Because you will be more alert to ministry needs that conform to your own gifts.

Recently, I asked a group of lay pastors in our church, "What are the greatest needs in this church?" You can guess what happened. Those who had the gift of evangelism began talking about the need for greater outreach. Those with the gift of hospitality began to talk about the need to open up our homes to those in need. Those with the gift of teaching began to highlight the instructional needs that exist within our fellowship. You see, when one examines the needs within a fellowship, that one tends to see those needs that will best utilize the gifts he or she has.

The need, however, does not constitute the call. Because I observe a particular need in a fellowship does not mean that I must respond to it. There are some people who, if they responded to every need they saw, would quickly be overcommitted. People who are overcommitted to church ministries are candidates to become burned out. These are people who have simply overcommitted themselves for various reasons and now refuse to be involved in any ministry. A warning needs to be sounded especially to those with the gifts of helps and serving. They tend to see many needs around them and quickly become overcommitted.

Let's look at *step four*. The key word here is "results" or "track record." What have been the results or the fruit of your ministry? John Wesley used to ask his lay preachers several questions before he would accept them into active ministry. The first pertained to their conversion. The second one dealt with the call of God on their lives. The third pertained to their gifts and graces for this ministry. Finally he wanted to know about the fruit of their ministry. Had they been effective? Had they seen positive results coming from the exercise of their gifts?

May I suggest an exercise for you to measure the results of your ministry? Make a list of all the ministries in which you have been engaged. Beside each one of these ministries, write down a number—one through five. A five would mean that you had excellent results; four, that you had good results; three, that you had fair results; two, that you had poor results; and one, meaning "let's not talk about it." By doing this exercise, you should be able to find those ministries in which you have been most effective. Then you need to ask the question, "What gifts was I using in those ministries?"

The *fifth step* in finding your spiritual gifts is the guidance of the Holy Spirit. How is He leading you right now? Do you sense any particular open doors or, for that matter, even closed doors of ministry? Is He exposing you to some new ministry that you find meaningful and exciting? If so, that may give you a further glimpse into some of the gifts that you have. I don't know how

God leads you in the decisions you make, but the way He has chosen to lead me in much of my life is by the open-door policy. Certain doors tend to open, and open wide, while other doors remain inflexibly locked. That is one of the ways that God has chosen to lead our lives.

Finally, let us consider the *sixth step* for finding your gifts. The key word here is "community." By "community" we mean the community of faith—our brothers and sisters, the church. If you were to ask several of your closest acquaintances in your fellowship to evaluate the gifts that you have, what would they say? It might be that they would affirm certain gifts by saying, "Say, Debbie, you remember when you led that Sunday School class? That was outstanding. Your teaching was so helpful to all of us, and you were so easy to listen to." That would be their way of affirming your gift.

Or you might hear this, "Say, Dave, I understand you are thinking about teaching our Sunday School class on a regular basis. Can I share something with you as a fellow member in Christ? Dave, I have seen you operate in several different ministries. I have watched you as you worked with the visitation teams here at the church, and you and I both know how effective you have been in that area. Dave, if I have any understanding of your gifts, it seems to me that your gifts would be much more effectively utilized by continuing to work on the visitation team rather than by teaching the Sunday School class. I am not sure whether or not you have the gift of teaching, but I am convinced that you have the gift of evangelism, and you have used it so effectively on our visitation team."

Would it be hard for Dave's friend to share that with him? Yes, it would be. Most of us are not conditioned to sharing so candidly with our Christian brothers and sisters. But Dave's friend has just done him a great service by telling him that evidence of Dave's having the gift of teaching is not visible. If Dave listens carefully to his friend, it could spare him a great amount of pain and anguish. All of us want to be used where we can maximize the gifts God has given us.

If you use the six steps suggested for finding your gifts, you may find the following questions helpful:

1. Are you open to be used by God for His service? _____

2. What are your goals/aspirations for ministry and service? _____

3. What are the greatest needs you see in your local congregation now? _____

4. What are some of the ways you have ministered and served? _____

5. At this point of your spiritual pilgrimage, do you sense that the Holy Spirit has confirmed any particular gifts in your life as you walk in obedience to Him? Think about it a moment and list ways the Holy Spirit may be revealing your gifts to you. _____

_____

6. Have other Christians (who know you well) affirmed certain gifts in you? _____

VI. YOUR GIFT, MINISTRY, AND PERSONALITY

One important area of training is helping laypersons understand how their personalities relate to their ministries.

The relationship between gifts and personality profiles is important. Two persons with the gift of evangelism, for example, may manifest that gift in different ways, based upon their personalities. If the gift is the "what," the personality profile reveals the "how." An individual's personality profile will indicate how he or she will accomplish a task. When we recognize the difference of personalities, we will more clearly appreciate the fact that other people may minister in a style different from our own, even though they possess the same gift. In summary, the personality profile indicates how you will utilize the gift that God has given you.

When we are aware of not only the uniqueness of our gifts but also the unique ways in which we deploy them, we will avoid the error of assuming that others need to do their ministry our way. It is important for us to be aware of the uniqueness of our gifts and the unique ways we deploy them. This awareness can keep us from criticizing those who have similar gifts but different ministries. Some have mistakenly assumed that other persons should have the same gifts they have and that others should use the gift in the same way they do.

Let me illustrate. Suppose we were training a group of laypersons. Some of the laypersons have the personality trait of dominance. Others have the trait of conformity. Those with a high dominance tendency want to do the job right but in their own way. In contrast, those with a high conformity trait tend to be interested in detail. They give attention to minute guidelines. They like to have everything written out for them. It is important to tailor the training to fit their personalities. Different laypersons could have the same gift, but their personalities cause them to exhibit that gift in very different ways.

It is important to always tailor the training to accommodate the variety of God's people. It is important, layperson, in selecting a ministry, that you find a ministry that not only utilizes your gifts but also allows you sufficient latitude to carry out that ministry in a way that conforms to your basic personality traits.

DISCUSSION QUESTIONS

1. What are some of the dangers related to the study of spiritual gifts?

2. How should we differentiate between talents and gifts?

3. What guidelines do we have to help us discover our spiritual gifts?

4. Why should we not expect all persons to have the same spiritual gifts?

5. If you have discovered your spiritual gifts, how did you make that discovery?

6. How do you see a study of spiritual gifts contributing to the growth of your church?

Called
Gifted
Trained
Sent

5
Training for Ministry

I. PLANS FOR LAY TRAINING

If laypersons are to be involved in fruitful ministry, training is essential. Many times I have seen pastors ask laypersons to fulfill important roles in the church without offering them any training opportunities—that is unfair.

A properly balanced view of lay ministry stresses not only the *call to* ministry and the *gifts for* ministry but also *training for* ministry. Any person who takes the ministry of the laity seriously must give adequate attention to training. Ministry is not automatic. It may not always require strict regimentation, but it does need avenues for training and expression.

Over the past few years I have observed numerous churches and their training programs. I am convinced that in many local churches, training for laypersons for their ministry is an extremely low priority. If we are to take lay ministry seriously, training will need to have a priority it has not had in most of our churches in the past. Lay training must be "intentional." Much of what has been labeled lay training has been done by default rather than by design. Lay ministry training needs to happen on purpose. It must be designed with clear objectives, goals, and methods. The layperson is not trained for ministry as a side job.

Several years ago the pastor of Bethany First Church of the Nazarene, Ponder W. Gilliland, drew up a list of priorities for the eight years between 1978 and 1986. Here are the five points of the "Mission of the Church":

1. *To be a worshiping congregation* (where we as the Body of Christ gather close to one another and to Him to be touched by Him, to touch Him and one another in depth).
2. *To be a* healing *fellowship* (where there is a ministry to the whole person toward helping each person find wholeness).
3. *To be an equipping center* (where the laity discover their gifts for ministry and are equipped for it).
4. *To be an evangelizing agency* (to touch the people of central Oklahoma with the good news of Jesus Christ, and to invite them to respond to His love).
5. *To be a deployment agency* (to send our people into the world of central Oklahoma living out the life of Christ as persons *forgiven and forgiving, loved and loving, cared for and caring*).

Notice how many of the five points of the "Mission of the Church" speak to the issue of lay training. Numbers 3, 4, and 5 specifically call for a meaningful training program. This pastor made lay development the priority item over that eight-year period. Lay training, if it is to occur, will have to occur on purpose, by design. Tragically, few congregations have systematic, well-developed, clearly thought-out methods to train laypeople for their ministries.

Some people object to the term "lay training." They believe the word "training" makes it sound as though ministry is something extraneous to the nature of the *laos,* the people of God. Thus they prefer the term "laity formation." Another reason some prefer to use the words "laity formation" is that they fear the old division between laity and clergy will recur if the clergy's role is referred to as training. They feel it is condescending for one person to say he or she is training another.

According to A. W. Kist, "Modern lay training . . . does not consist of one-track communication of thoughts between the leader and his audience."[1] Lay training or lay formation is far more interactional than that. At the core of lay training are two presuppositions: first, that the people of God exist for service for which they need training; and second, that those who train them are their servants, not their masters. When we talk about lay ministry training, we are not talking about persons who desire to lord their knowledge over those who do not know. Rather, we are talking about laypersons who want to be all God would have them to be and who need "equippers." These equippers are usually pastors who can help them understand their call to ministry, discover their gifts for ministry, learn how to select that ministry, and provide some kind of training for that ministry.

It might be well for you to analyze the present lay ministry training program in your fellowship. Below are a series of questions that will help you determine not only the extent of your current training but also your needs for training laypersons. Answer the questions below:

Lay Training Questionnaire

1. In what ways are laity being taught their "call" to ministry?

_____

_____

_____

2. What training has been provided for laypersons in gift discovery? _____

_____

3. What ministries are available for those with particular gifts?

_____

_____

4. Is a comprehensive list of lay ministry opportunities available to all laypersons? _____

5. Are laity given thorough training for the ministries in which they are involved? _____

6. List the lay ministries in the local church and the training provided:

Ministry	Training	Length of Training
_____	_____	_____
_____	_____	_____
_____	_____	_____
_____	_____	_____
_____	_____	_____
_____	_____	_____

7. In what ministries are laity inadequately trained for ministry? What can be done to improve training?

Ministry   Potential Training

_____   _____

_____   _____

_____   _____

_____   _____

_____   _____

8. What persons have the gifts and skills to facilitate the potential training mentioned in number 7?

Ministry   Person

_____   _____

_____   _____

_____   _____

_____   _____

II. The Equipper and the Training Process

While I was speaking in a seminar on lay ministry several years ago, one pastor became upset at what I was saying. He felt that if I told laypersons that they were ministers and that they were to be trained to have their own ministries, we would soon do away with the need for pastors. I thought about his words a great deal and wondered why he so badly misunderstood what I was saying. From that point I changed the focus of the seminar. Rather than speaking of the ministry of the laity, I began talking about *partnership*—pastor and layperson as *partners* in ministry. That is how the title of this book was born.

Any serious view of the ministry of the laity assumes an important role for the pastors. A high doctrine of the laity is based upon an equally high doctrine of the clergy. For laypersons to have effective ministries, they must be assisted and directed in those ministries. Who provides that for them? Who equips them? Who enables them? Obviously that is their pastor's role. The pastor is the one who underscores the biblical call to ministry. The pastor is the one who helps them understand the gifts and leads them through the steps of finding their gifts. It is their pastor who instructs or at least administers the training by which they can become effective ministers. Every effective lay minister depends upon the training and encouragement provided by his or her pastor. *Ministry of the laity is not some reactionary, anticlergy movement. It is, in contrast to that, a movement to bring laypersons into a closer working relationship with their pastors!*

A. *Guidelines for Equippers*

Some have concluded that lay ministry meant that professional church workers will somehow become unnecessary. Not so. Pastors, separated by their function, not by status, are called to teach the Word with such clarity that laypersons understand their calls to ministry and discover their gifts for ministry. The clergy or pastors provide the channels in which laypersons are trained and equipped for ministry.

The clergy are not *the* ministers. They are *trainers* of ministers. The congregation does not consist of 1 minister and 200 parishioners; rather it consists of 200 potential ministers (or ministering laypersons) and 1 equipper (or pastoral minister). One is called to the ministry of enablement, but all are called to minister. Thus, a high view of lay ministry recognizes the importance of the clergy, for it is the clergy who facilitate lay ministry. Any layperson who believes the ministry of the laity does away with his pastor does not understand the crucial role of the equipper. Any pastor who feels that ministry of the laity is not really all that important is failing to understand the call God has placed on the *laos*, the people of God.

Edwin Linberg wrote his doctoral dissertation on the clergy as equippers. In it he noted that

> when the clergy operate as enablers, the laity will take responsibility for their ministry as part of God's people, the Church. . . . The clergy who will risk himself or herself in a ministry of equipping laity for ministry, will not be disappointed with the results. There will be satisfaction with the laity's ability to do effective work in the ministry. There will be personal feelings of accomplishment in the exercise of their professional skills to equip laity for ministry.[2]

Linberg further noted that a pastor who conscientiously practices ministry as an equipper is marked by the following:

> 1. He or she is thoroughly knowledgeable and articulate concerning the various dimensions of ministry, biblically, theologically, and practically; 2. He or she is equipped with the skills necessary to involve persons in the processes of experiential learning; 3. He or she employs those skills as creatively as is possible in every situation, relationship, encounter, and activity in the life of the congregation they serve, since every situation and relationship is a potential opportunity for learning and growth; 4. He or she sees the basic role of a professional minister being a "link" or "bridge" by which people move from intellectual and verbal assent to the idea that they are responsible for the ministry of Christ to the actual practice of their ministry in the world as God's people; and, 5. He or she disciplines the exercising of their ministry so that every phase of it is directed to increasing the ministry of the laity, thereby expanding the impact of Christ's ministry through the lives of others.[3]

Several basic guidelines for equippers will help us as pastors in training laypersons for their ministries.

1. One simple guideline is to encourage persons in our congregation to use terms properly. We talked about this in chapter 1. Take the term "minister," for example. If laypersons refer to one person in the congregation as *the* minister, they will assume that they, the laypersons, are not ministers. Perhaps we should encourage our people to use the term "minister" in a more biblical perspective. All of us are ministers. We certainly understand that we are called to different ministries. As the clergy, we are called to pastoral ministry; as laypersons, we are called to various lay ministries. The important thing is to understand that all are truly ministers in the biblical sense of that term.

2. Another guideline for the equipper is the importance of affirming the vocational ministries. We have stated previously that all laypersons are responsible not only for their churchly ministries but for their vocational ministries as well. Since we as pastors are so involved in our work in the church, we can easily forget that the laypersons live not only in the world of the church but also in the world of the world at the same time. They live with pressures and stresses that we tend to forget.

3. Equippers should evaluate all church activities for their

equipping potential. How many activities in your fellowship specifically equip your people for their ministries? What functions more correspond to the nature of the church than equipping laypersons to be the *laos?*

4. Equippers should select persons with gifts and skills who can assist them in equipping others. I have had to ask other people to help me with the training process. Our minister of pastoral care has assisted me in training lay pastors in certain areas. He helps equip them in the areas of hospital visitation and ministry to families who have just experienced the death of a loved one. Another capable leader has trained our lay pastors in counseling. He has taught them how to refer the counselee to appropriate counselors and how to be creative listeners. A successful businessman in our congregation has given training to our lay pastors on counseling the financially troubled. All of these persons are specialists in their areas, offering more expertise in their respective fields than I can. Every congregation has talented laypersons who can assist the pastor in the equipping process. Although we refer to the pastor as the equipper, it might be more accurate to say that he or she is to see that equipping is done. Gifted laypersons assist in the equipping process.

5. Another guideline for equippers is to be certain that the training process includes doing. How many of us have gone through training processes that included only classroom experience, only to find out that actual doing is much more difficult than we anticipated. Any training process must include a balance between classroom experience and on-the-job experience.

Several years ago I was an associate pastor in a church where I trained three groups of laity to be lay pastors. The first group was in training almost eight months before they began functioning as lay pastors. Group two was in training about four or five months before they began functioning as lay pastors. Group three started working as lay pastors when they were only one month old as a group. Why did I speed up this process? Well, I made an interesting discovery. One day as the lay pastors in group one were coming together for a training session, one of them said, "You know, we have enjoyed being together like this so much, let's just keep meeting forever and not worry about becoming lay pastors." That was a clue to me that I had allowed them the privilege of the classroom experience too long without giving them on-the-job experience. They were enjoying each other's company, but I had failed to whet their appetites for actual ministering to other people. Any effective training program must include doing, not merely classroom experience.

B. *The Training Process*

A training process involves at least five distinct stages.[4] The equipper must understand balance between these stages. The first one is *association*. That means simply being with the people you are training. People who are trained for meaningful lay ministry will work in direct proportion to their commitment to you as a person, their equipper. Thus, the training process involves much more than conveying cognitive knowledge of the "how-tos" of ministry. Effective lay ministry training begins with the bonding of a close relationship between the equipper and the one being equipped.

The second stage is *impartation*. This is the actual communication of the basic "how-tos" of that ministry. This stage of training might be nicknamed "the classroom stage."

The third stage is *demonstration*. Few people learn by being told what to do. Almost everyone learns by watching another person do it. I did not learn how to share my faith by hearing a sermon on the need to witness. I learned by watching one of my colleagues share his faith. I watched him do it again and again and again. Finally, it became a part of my own lifestyle.

A fourth stage in the training process is *delegation*. That means assigning it. This may be hard for some pastors to do. But it is important to assign a ministry to a layperson and allow him or her the freedom to fail as well as to succeed. In this stage, it is important that the layperson understand that if the ministry is to be done at all, it will be done by him or her. No pastor trains laypeople well by giving them the impression that the pastor will be picking up the tabs any time the laypeople fail to do their ministry.

The fifth stage is *supervision*. This means overseeing it. It is necessary to develop lines of accountability, methods for monitoring the ministry that is being done. The purpose for establishing these lines of accountability is not to police the lay ministers. It is to encourage them, assist them in whatever way will be most helpful.

III. Overcoming Obstacles for Lay Ministry Training

There are several barriers that can prevent a church from beginning lay ministry training programs. Let's talk about some of them. Maybe we should meet separately right now. By that I mean, let's separate all of you pastors from all of you laypersons who are reading this book. Right now we are going to ask some questions about lay ministry training. Pastors, you will read the responses under "Pastors' Answer." Laypersons, you will read the responses under "Laypersons' Answer." Now don't let me catch anyone reading from the wrong section! We will blow the whistle and start all over if you do that.

What are the obstacles?

Obstacle Number One: Some pastors feel threatened at the thought of lay ministry.

Pastors' Answer:

Pastors, it is easy for us to confuse two distinct things: "Liberation of the laity" means liberating laypersons to ministry, not liberating them to anarchy. Some pastors who fear a significant emphasis on the ministry of the laity assume that their laypersons will become unnecessarily assertive in the life of the church. This is not at all what we are suggesting. Lay ministry means liberating laypersons to utilize their gifts. This will not detract from your ministry. In fact, the doing of all this is the fulfillment of your ministry. In reality, your ministry will be multiplied many items over to the extent that you train and equip your laypersons for their own service to God. There is no need for pastors to be threatened by the thought of lay ministry.

Laypersons' Answer:

Laypersons, one of the reasons pastors sometimes feel threatened is because they have known of churches where laypersons became so assertive that the pastor was given no opportunity to exercise gifts of leadership. This is most unfortunate. One of the ways to make certain that you do not threaten your pastor by asking for training in lay ministry is by letting your pastor know that you desire to partner with him or her in ministry. Let your pastor know you need help in understanding better what your gifts are and how to use them. In so doing, you will utilize to the maximum not only your gifts but your pastor's gifts as well. And you will sense that you have a pastor who not only is not threatened but also is fulfilled. In its plainest terms, you will enjoy your relationship with him or her.

Obstacle Number Two: Some pastors may feel inadequate to provide training in lay ministry.

Pastors' Answer:

Pastors, this is understandable. We need to admit that with all of our Bible college and undergraduate training and our seminary education, *most of us have not received adequate training in how to train our laypersons for their ministries.* We have been taught to be *professional clergy* but not how to train *others* to minister. It is not at all strange that we should feel inadequate. I have been to five educational institutions during my ministerial training. Though all were good institutions and were schools that I am proud to have been associated with, I received little training in *how to train others.* I am learning as I go.

One of the best things we as pastors can do is to be honest. When we try to fulfill a particular ministry and we struggle with feelings of inadequacy, it is good to admit it. I don't hesitate to tell our lay pastors that I am not certain of the best way to train them. I am experimenting. Any time one experiments, there will be trial and error—particularly error. I ask them to be patient with me, because it will take me time to learn how to best equip and train them for their ministry.

What are we saying? There is nothing wrong with feeling inadequate for the training process. That is understandable. However, laypersons might not be understanding if we attempt to deny or disguise our inadequacies. It is much better to admit them and to begin to strive to improve our ability to train others for ministry.

Laypersons' Answer:

Laypersons, you need to understand the importance of being patient with us pastors. Some of us have not had a great deal of training in how to train *you* for *ministry.* If you will give us enough time and allow us the freedom to fail in our experiments, we will learn how to better train you. In other words, I am asking you to be patient with us. We will appreciate it, because we truly desire to learn how to better train you for your respective ministries.

We don't deny the fact that we often feel inadequate in training you for ministry. Remember that this emphasis upon ministry of the laity is new to many of us. It was stressed very little in our academic training. Thus, we have much learning and, in some cases, re-learning to do to really put it into practice in our churches.

Obstacle Number Three: Some pastors may feel that lay training is unnecessary.

Pastors' Answer:

I am going to ask Edwin Linberg to respond to this obstacle from his dissertation.

As I began this project, I traced my personal experience in the professional ministry from seminary and student church days, through my first pastorate, and into the position I have now held for six and one half years, pastor of Temple City Church, Temple City, California. The reflections upon my experience were laid over against my feelings about the thrust for the renewal of the church which has been prominent in the church during the past two decades, at least in its writing and speaking.

My basic conviction, growing out of this process, was that church renewal has not happened to the extent desired or dreamed of because of the inability and/or the unwillingness of the clergy to enable it to happen. The clergy, through either lack of skill or deliberate choice, have not provided the training needed by the laity to fully exercise their ministry. If training was not needed, they have not freed-up the opportunities for the laity to be involved in the ministry. As I began this project, I felt the thrust for church renewal had been more hindered by the clergy than by the laity's difficulty with ministry or their failure to assume responsibility for it.

Building on this conviction, I stated this as my thesis, "If the laity, the whole people of God, are going to accept the responsibility for ministry, in light of the biblical heritage which proclaims ministry to be that responsibility of the whole people of God, the clergy must become enablers, equipping the laity for ministry."[5]

Linberg's words are not easy to bear. He is suggesting that *the "problem of the laity" is really not a problem of the laity at all. It's the "problem of the clergy!"* We have not willingly provided the training that laypersons have needed in order for them to be involved in meaningful, systematic, consistent ministry. It is far easier for us as pastors to *say* that lay ministry is important than it is for us to *take action* that provides opportunities for training our laypeople. I have yet to find a single pastor who does not verbally espouse the importance of the ministry of the laity. Yet I can take you to numerous churches that do not provide any kind of nurturing process for laypersons to be involved in a fulfilling ministry. We have not placed it high enough on our priorities.

Laypersons' Answer:

Laypersons, this is one of the most difficult obstacles we could ever put in your pathway. If your pastor is not persuaded that lay ministry is of crucial importance, frankly there is very little you can do. I have been invited on several occasions to speak to groups of laypeople at seminars on the topic of lay ministry. I am hesitant to do that because I know there is always the possibility that some laypersons may go back to their local church excited about possibilities of their ministry, only to find a pastor who is considerably less excited.

Most laypersons are fortunate if they have pastors who really want to see the laity trained for ministry. However, on occasion, laypersons find themselves in the position where they are not encouraged in any way to be involved in ministry.

If your pastor feels that lay ministry training is unnecessary, I would encourage you to: (1) sincerely pray for your pastor; (2) make appointments with your pastor to share your concern; (3) do not give up on your pastor (we pastors have been known to change, you know); (4) do not become a crusader; don't attempt to rally other people around you in some kind of an antipastor crusade; (5) learn the spiritual grace of waiting.

I am aware that it is easier for me to *say* these things to you than for me to *do* them; but I believe that if they are followed, they will pay high dividends. And they will increase the chances that you will produce the desired results.

Obstacle Number Four: Some laypersons feel threatened by lay ministry training.

Pastors' Answer:

Pastors, some of us are going to hear laypersons say, "What is all this talk about ministry? I'm not a minister! You are the minister! That's what we pay you for." The laypersons will say, according to Dr. James Kennedy, "Let Ecclesiastical George do it! That's what he is paid for!" Some laypersons are simply going to be frightened at the idea that they are ministers and they have ministries. If that is the case, it is important that we give them plenty of emotional elbow room. Give them time.

Move with the movers. Work with those who are *not* threatened by it. Allow those who are threatened to see meaningful lay ministry operating around them. This will do more to dissolve their fears than any words we might say. Putting it simply, be patient and find those who will work with you in significant ministry training activities. In time, those who are threatened will learn to feel more secure with the idea that they are ministers as well.

Laypersons' Answer:

Laypersons, some of you are probably not the least bit threatened by discussion on the ministry of the laity. But some of your brothers and sisters are. If you fall into that category, it is important that you admit to your pastor your hesitancy to be involved in ministry. Perhaps there has been a time in your past when you have tried some particular ministry and have failed. Or maybe you have been involved in some ministry that has been disappointing and discouraging. For some reason in your past, you find the thought of lay ministry either frightening or revolting.

Whatever the case, may I encourage you to do something? Would you set up a personal appointment with your pastor and talk with him or her about it? Share your concern. Share your feelings. Even though it may be hard for you to do, I recommend that you try one more time. Ask the pastor to figuratively "take you by the hand and walk you through the training process." Tell your pastor that you need assistance very much as you begin being involved in ministry.

Your fear is probably normal, but don't let your fear of being involved in ministry cripple you and prevent you from being all that God wants you to be. You have been uniquely gifted by Him for a specific ministry within the kingdom of God. Make yourself available to your pastor so that you can find your gifts and begin to experiment with ministry. Remember, there is no wrong in failing. It is in failure that we most often discover how to succeed.

Obstacle Number Five: Some laypersons may feel inadequate.

Pastors' Answer:

Pastors, this should be easy for us all to understand. Most laypersons have been in no training program for the ministry you are asking them to do. Think back for a moment, pastors, to when you preached your first sermons. Most of you had at least some training, and yet you were still fearful. Many of you have had four years of undergraduate training and three years of seminary. Yet those first few weeks at that first church were terrifying. Why? It was a new experience.

Many laypeople have even more reason to be frightened of various ministries simply because they have received no training. They have been asked to do certain jobs and have been given little help in assuming them. Bear in mind that not all laypersons are going to feel inadequate. Some are going to feel overconfident. But you will discover some who will say, "I can't do that. That is just too big of a job for me." What they are saying is, "I need training and I need help. Can you provide that for me?"

The danger for us as pastors is that we might misinterpret their words and assume that they are unwilling to be involved in ministry. Normally that is not the case. When they say no to ministry, they are often saying no because they feel like they just don't know how to do the things they are supposed to do.

One clue that they are feeling inadequate is when you hear these words: "But I'm only a layperson." Those words should be a signal to you of feelings of inadequacy and the need for careful, systematic training. As you will recall from a previous chapter, the success of the Methodist movement was based on an army of simple, plain laypersons, adequately trained, properly motivated, accomplishing a mighty work for God. There is no layperson in your congregation who cannot have a meaningful place in the total ministry of the Body of Christ.

Laypersons' Answer:

Laypersons, it is normal for you to feel inadequate. All of us, when we begin something new, have those kinds of feelings. Paul Cladell, in *The Satin Slipper,* made the following statement: "God writes straight with crooked lines." What I think he is trying to say is that God is able to work through all of us, regardless of our inadequacies. You will find it very fulfilling as He works through you. Your feelings of inadequacy only give Him more opportunity to demonstrate the effective way in which He can work through you.

What will make you effective as a lay minister is not the extent of your talents or feelings of adequacy but the extent to which you open yourself to Him, so that He can work through you. If you are struggling, layperson, with strong feelings of inadequacy about being involved in meaningful lay ministry, talk to your pastor. Let your pastor know of your willingness to be involved, but assure him or her of how inadequate you may feel. You will find your pastor to be understanding. Your pastor can help you. Your pastor *will* help you. As pastors, *we are not, first of all, looking for people who feel they are adequate. We look for people who are willing.* Let your pastor know you are that kind of person. Confidence and competence will come later on in the training process. Then feelings of inadequacy will begin to disappear.

Obstacle Number Six: Some laypersons may feel that training is unnecessary.

Pastors' Answer:

I recall on one occasion attempting to take a layperson to a witnessing clinic that was sponsored by Campus Crusade for Christ. To my knowledge, this man, though a dedicated man, had never spoken to anyone about his faith in Christ. Yet at the same time, he expressed a desire to be used of God in this area. I felt the witnessing clinic would really help him. When I asked him if he would go with me to the training program, he responded, "There is nothing that they could teach me that I don't already know."

What was his problem? I'm not sure. It might have been that he was simply threatened at the thought of going to another church and receiving training from a group of people with whom he was unfamiliar. I think the problem, however, was simply a sense of exaggerated over-confidence. He did not know how to share his faith that well. Yet he saw training as essentially unnecessary.

What can we as pastors do when we come up against this obstacle? In some cases it is probably best to go ahead and allow the layperson to move into that field of ministry and not force the issue. It is difficult to fill a need that a person is not consciously aware of. As soon as the layperson expresses a desire for or an awareness of the need for training, then you can begin to talk to him or her about a structured training program.

There is a danger in handling this problem this way. Sometimes laypersons who refuse any kind of training will find themselves experiencing difficulties. It is not much fun picking up the pieces in those cases. However, there are times when it is worth taking the risk. I certainly don't want to give you the impression that all laypersons who fail to be excited about training do so because they are overconfident. Some simply do not yet know the value of training. They will begin to get excited about it if they will simply begin to take training for their ministry.

I also want to acknowledge that some persons do not appear to need much training. Extremely talented laypersons from time to time may find themselves with the ability to move into almost any ministry and experience good results. Though these situations are rare, they still need to be acknowledged. Not all laypersons want to be trained. But many do.

The task as a pastor is not so much to persuade people of the need for training, as it is to provide the opportunities for training to those laypersons who are already aware of the need. If laypersons are excited about their call to ministry and have an awareness of their gifts for ministry, it is not uncommon that they will come to an awareness of the need for a tool-sharpening process—a time of training.

Laypersons' Answer:

Probably most of you do not identify closely with this obstacle. Most of you, as active laypersons, really do desire to be equipped as well as possible for your ministry. But there are some of you who tend to be resistant. This makes it difficult for us as pastors to assist you. You may feel like there are times when you know more about a particular ministry than we do. In some cases, you are probably right. But in most cases, you will discover that your pastor, by virtue of his experience and his exposure to many other church situations, can greatly assist you.

There may be another reason why some of you would resist training. It is stated in an alarming quote from Arnold Come:

> Sociologists are insisting that the majority of church members are interested only in what the church can do in ministering to their personal needs . . . the "caretaker" role of the church. And those pastors who are anxious to train the laity for mission in the world, and who organize such training programs, soon find they have two congregations—the minority who respond, and the majority who strongly resist such a "new" interpretation for the reason for the church's existence.[6]

In other words, too many laypersons, according to the above statement, desire to be the recipients of ministry rather than ministers themselves. This condition can only be changed when laypersons come to the full awareness of what God desires for their lives. We want you as laypersons to know that we as pastors desire to assist and help you in any way we can.

When we talk about lay training, we are not referring to a monological arrangement where the pastor does all of the talking and you as the laypersons do all of the listening. We are talking instead about the quality of a relationship between people who are committed to the same objective—that objective being to equip and enable you to enjoy the most fruitful ministry possible. In other words, the reason we as pastors want to persuade you that training is important is because you have been profoundly gifted by God and we want you to experience all the fulfillment that you possibly can in the utilization of those gifts.

IV. FINDING THE APPROPRIATE MINISTRY

We have talked at length about the obstacles of lay ministry. But once we have hurdled these obstacles, what do we do? How do we help people select the proper ministry? How do we select that particular ministry that best utilizes our gift? Before one can be trained, he or she must make that selection. It is not uncommon for a person to try several areas of ministry before discovering one that utilizes his or her gift to the maximum. Admittedly, one may experience some failure while in the process of discovering that particular ministry in which he or she can best function. One of the simplest ways to begin the selection process is to take a sheet of paper and jot down every ministry that you can think of that would utilize your gift. (See diagram below.)

My Gift: _teaching_

Ministries that will utilize my gift:

1. Sunday School teacher
2. Home Bible Study teacher
3. Youth Camp
4. Vacation Bible School

To aid you in discovering your ministry, I would recommend Tim Blanchard's book *A Practical Guide to Finding Your Spiritual Gifts*.[7] Here Tim had listed many of the gifts, after which he has made a list of numerous ministries that would use that gift. (Note Appendix A. It is taken from Tim Blanchard's book.) Many laypersons might find it difficult to list all of the ministries that could utilize their gifts. It is helpful to talk to your pastor, who can help you discover the ministry that would best suit the gift God has given you. You can also use another method to find your proper ministry. This method works in reverse. Get a list of all of the volunteer ministry positions in your church.

MINISTRIES:

Sunday School Superintendent
Sunday School Treasurer
Sunday School Secretary
Church Board Member
Usher
Greeter
Nursery Worker
Bible Study Leader
Bible Study Host

As you go through the list, write which gifts are needed to fill those ministry positions. Or take that ministry list and simply write down all the ministries listed there that could use your gift or gifts. Admittedly, this is finding your ministry by reduction, but it often works. After you have selected those ministries that you think might best use your gifts, go to the persons who oversee those ministries. In some cases this will be your pastor. Ask for counsel. Find out if your pastor sees you as having the particular gifts necessary to fill the ministry you have marked on the list.

"Finding My Place" Seminar

Several years ago I was an associate pastor at a church where we offered a "finding my place" seminar. The goals of this seminar were to help laypersons: (1) understand their call to ministry; (2) understand their gifts of ministry; (3) be familiar with the volunteer ministry positions in the church; (4) learn how to manage their time in such a way that they could be involved in ministry; (5) know the directors of the various ministries of our church; and (6) enlist in at least one area of ministry so they could begin to experiment in the use of their gifts.

V. Steps of Laity Training

What are the basic ingredients of a lay training program? While the following is not a complete list of steps for training your laypersons for ministry, here are some of the stages I believe are useful. (1) Highlight the call to ministry. (2) Assist laypersons in isolating their gift or gifts for ministry. (3) Find creative ways of assisting laypersons to select the ministry that will best utilize their gift(s). (4) Expose your lay ministers to all available literature on the topic. For example, if some have a gift of evangelism, there are many well-written books they should know about. If some have a gift of helps, you might expose them to chapter 3 of Barbara Kuhn's book on lay ministry (Barbara Kuhn, *The Whole Lay Ministry Catalog* [New York: Seabury Press, 1979]). There are also helpful books written that affirm strongly the doctrine of vocations. One of the most outstanding is Elton Trueblood's *Your Other Vocation* (New York: Harper and Brothers, 1952). Another book of particular interest to businesspeople is Orley Heron's *A Christian Executive in a Secular World* (Nashville: Thomas Nelson Publishers, 1979). There is much good literature available to assist laypersons in their training process. (The *Leader's Guide* Appendix, Item I provides a more complete list.)

(5) If possible, each new lay minister should function as an apprentice to a more experienced layperson who is working in the same ministry. Often laypersons who are asked to fill certain ministry positions are thrust into them with little supervision and guidance. Having a more experienced lay minister alongside assures the younger lay minister of a more fruitful ministry. Simply put, lay ministry needs demonstration and supervision.

Pioneer Bishop Francis Asbury is said to have trained some 5,000 lay preachers during the frontier years of Methodism in America. On one occasion someone asked him how he trained his lay preachers. To that he responded, "I show them the way." And show them the way he did! He embarked on a journey by horseback that took him to and fro across the frontier many, many times.[8]

(6) Form support groups or ministry modules. The term "module" is borrowed from David Mains's *Full Circle*.[9] A module is simply a group of persons who have come together with interest in a similar ministry. There are two techniques for training people. One I call the "transient bus" theory. According to this theory an arbitrary group of people sit side by side and happen to be going the same direction for a short period of time. They remain essentially strangers to each other. The second technique I call the family theory. This theory says that it is better to train people as a circle of persons who are conscious of a close kinship

with one another. In the "transient bus" theory, the only thing that the people have in common is the fact that they are going the same direction for a brief period of time. The family theory places the people in a circle face-to-face, interacting with one another. (The above theories were adapted from W. H. Fitchett's *Wesley and His Century*.)[10]

It is important as we train laity for their ministries that they see themselves as being a part of a larger organization. They need to know they are a part of an ongoing movement that not only is bigger than themselves but also will outlast themselves. They need to be face-to-face with other people who are likewise attempting to use their gifts in ministry. They need to know what it is to share the joy of ministry. They also need to share some of the hurts involved in lay ministry. Admittedly the "transient bus" theory is easier. In this method people simply assemble themselves in a room and look forward at a trainer. The important thing is not the student but the content being set forth. That method usually does not produce long-term results. The success of our lay ministry training is directly proportional to the extent that we build close bonds between the trained laity and the ones who are doing the training. It has been aptly noted that Methodism's early effectiveness in England was directly related to its small groups. This concept is as essential for us in the 20th century as it was for John Wesley in the 18th.

(7) Establish clear lines of accountability. There needs to be some method by which the equipper can evaluate the layperson's ministry. Some kind of evaluation form is needed if we are to successfully encourage the layperson in ministry. Several years ago I developed a successful ministry report card that lay pastors could turn in to me on a weekly basis. On that card the lay pastors indicated how many home visits and telephone contacts they had made during that week. They also indicated any hospital visits they had made, along with all other miscellaneous lay pastors' activities. There was also a place on the card for them to indicate what difficulties they might be encountering. The purpose of the card was not to produce guilt in those who failed to make their goal for the week but rather to serve as a tool to evaluate one's overall ministry effectiveness. A ministry report card form is only one of many ways to develop a proper line of

LAY PASTOR MINISTRY FORM

L.P. _____ Parish _____ NO. _____

Week Ending _____ Week No. _____

Goal: "2/6" YES ☐ NO ☐ (circle one)

Home Visits	Telephone Contacts	Hospital or "One-on-One" Contacts
1. _____	1. _____	1. _____
2. _____	2. _____	2. _____
_____	3. _____	3. _____
_____	4. _____	4. _____
_____	5. _____	
_____	6. _____	

Info to Minister of Pastoral Care: _____ Other L.P. Activities:

Turn in each Sunday morning.

ᶜ1980 James L. Garlow

107

accountability between the equipper and those who are being equipped.

With all this stress on training, it is possible to lose sight of the goal. Layperson, don't allow that to happen to you. You are being made ready for action. Remember Eph. 4? The purpose of lay ministry is to be all that a loving God desires us to be. That's my prayer, and I know it's yours too.

DISCUSSION QUESTIONS

1. How would you answer the person who considers a lay ministry program as an anticlergy movement?

2. What are the five distinct stages essential to an adequate lay training program?

3. In discussing Section III, "Overcoming Obstacles for Lay Ministry Training," select a member of your class to represent a pastor and another a layperson. Ask these two persons to summarize for your group the answers to the six obstacles to lay training as presented in this section of your text.

4. How would you differentiate between the "transient bus" theory and the family theory of lay training?

5. Why is modeling so important in the training of lay ministers?

6. What place does accountability play in the training of lay ministers?

6

Sent into Ministry

Ministry does not occur in isolation. It happens when we, as members of the Body of Christ—His Church—join our brothers and sisters in a mission into the world. We do not minister as individuals; we minister as members of something much greater than ourselves—the eternal Church of Jesus, the living Lord. Thus, when we as the *laos* set out on a ministry, we set out with the support of all who comprise the Church. The other members of the Body of Christ are vitally concerned with our ministry because it is done in the name of Jesus, the Head of the Church. Therefore, when we have completed our training, we are ready to receive the approval and blessings of our brothers and sisters in Christ—and to be sent for ministry.

I. Sent into the World

It should not surprise us that we should be sent forth into ministry. Our model of ministry—Jesus himself—was sent into ministry. In His prayer in John 17 He states that He had been sent into the world by God, the Father. In that same respect Jesus sent His followers into ministry. "I sent them into the world just as you sent me into the world" (John 17:18, TEV). On another occasion Jesus spoke to His disciples: "As the Father has sent me, I am sending you" (John 20:21).

In the accounts of the growth of the Early Church, certain persons were sent out. For example, Barnabas was sent by the church in Jerusalem. "A great number of people believed and turned to the Lord. News of this reached the ears of the church at Jerusalem, and they sent Barnabas to Antioch" (Acts 11:21-22). Paul and Barnabas were sent out by the church at Antioch. "While they [the church in Antioch] were worshiping the Lord and fasting, the Holy Spirit said, 'Set apart for me Barnabas and Saul [Paul] for the work to which I have called them.' So after they had fasted and prayed, they placed their hands on them and sent them off" (Acts 13:2-3).

Just as Barnabas and Paul and others were sent by the Early Church, you and I are likewise sent. We are sent by the church, sent into ministry. As believers we should perceive of our ministries in the light of the ministry of Christ. In the same manner that Christ is sent by the Father into the world to fulfill a special mission to humankind, so also should we as Christians understand ourselves to be sent to fulfill the mission with which we are entrusted. By being sent into ministry, we mean that as called, gifted, and trained laypersons, we are on a divine mission; we have a specific task. And as we do this task, we function as representatives of the sending party. We are representatives of the Church and of Jesus himself.

There is a difference between being called and being sent. Charles Lake carefully noted:

> Being called of God and being sent by God are two distinct operations of the Holy Spirit. The word "call," consistently used in the New Testament, is from a Greek word meaning "to call toward one's self, to summon." It is basically used in a three-fold manner: call to salvation, call to discipleship, and call to service. The word "send" is from a Greek word meaning "to send forth from one's self, furnished with credentials, with a commission to act as one's representative and accomplish a certain mission" (Wuest).
>
> Biblically speaking, God's call is not to go somewhere, but to be someone by His grace. It is in His sending that our direction is made known as to the geographical location . . . He calls us to himself in order that He might send us to others. Such is a very sound Biblical principle.[1]

We are sent as believers into the world to reclaim the world as God directs. Christians, you remember, exist not for themselves but for the world to which they are sent. Such is the nature of the meaning of the word *laos*, the people of God. As Kraemer noted, "Any accurate understanding of a theology of the Laity must begin with the fact that 'God is concerned about the world.'"[2] Perhaps no one has said it better than Hans-Ruedi Weber when he noted that every Christian needs two conversions. First, we need a conversion from the world to Christ. Second, we need a conversion to serve Christ in the world.[3] It is too easy for us to find ourselves, after conversion, so immersed in the world of the church that we forget about the world of the world. Perhaps the greatest threat of the Christian Church today is the threat of becoming ingrown, so focusing in on itself and its own needs that it fails to remember the purpose for which it was called into existence.

As laypersons you have a distinct advantage over us preacher types! You may never have realized this. The Christian layperson is strategically placed in the world with an accessibility to it that is denied to most pastors. In other words, you are able to have contact with the world in a way that few of the pastors can. The reason for that is probably obvious to you. You are accepted by your colleagues as fellow strugglers. In contrast we as pastors are often seen as semisaints, or at least we are placed on a pedestal. We are regarded as an elevated yet isolated group. As lay ministers you do not have that obstacle to overcome.[4]

Lay ministry is most effective when it is seen as a part of something larger than merely the individuals involved in that ministry. The apostle Paul stated it well. He said we're all a part of a Body. We function as cells within that Body. Lay ministry that is based upon a biblical view of the Church sees itself as a part of that Body. Lay ministry will be successful to the extent that support groups are built around each lay minister. The object of the sending group is not only to send but also to encourage the lay minister. How the group is formed or how it functions is less important than the fact that it does exist and that it does function.

Certainly support groups can be formed in many ways. One of the best ways is to bring people into a group of 10 or 12, all who have the same spiritual gift. As they meet from time to time, they can discuss the utilization of that particular gift. Though they will have different ministries, they certainly will have one common goal: to maximize the utilization of their gift for the purpose of advancing the cause of Christ. Another way a support group might be formed is by bringing together people with identical ministries. For example, a Sunday School teacher fills a crucial role in the church. Yet it is easy for a Sunday School teacher to see himself or herself as simply one person functioning in this ministry. If that teacher was brought together more often with other teachers for a time of sharing, building each other up in the faith, and encouraging each other in their service, how much more effective might that Sunday School teacher be.

The lay ministers within our churches need to come together at least once a month in order to evaluate their ministries. They can discuss any difficulties they have had. They can share concerns. They can laugh together over the joys and excitements of lay ministries that month. They may find themselves weeping together as they pray over the concerns of a particular lay minister. The purpose of that coming together is to help the lay ministers understand that they are a part of a larger unit of people. They are not simply individual lay ministers. They are serving on an exciting team. Much of the attrition experienced in lay ministry activities could be reduced if people did not experience such severe isolation. As pastors we frequently come together in groups and share our common concerns. Those are always times of great encouragement for us. Why should we expect any less for our lay ministers?

II. Setting Priorities

As pastors we need to assist our laypersons in setting priorities before they are commissioned to certain ministries. It is easy for all of us as Christians to live an unbalanced life and be unaware of it. Only by setting priorities and evaluating our lives in light of those priorities can we keep ourselves in proper balance. Beyond one's own personal spiritual life, the first priority for ministering laypersons should be the family. Almost all of us as pastors say that we believe our families should be first. The tragedy is that few people who say that actually do it! All of us have heard the tragic accounts of pastors who gave their lives to their congregations to the utter neglect of their own family members. All of us as pastors are vulnerable at this point. The problem is simple. We love our work and enjoy ministering to our congregations. We sense the depth of their needs, and in response to those needs we begin to give all our energy toward that one area of ministry. In the process we forget that our number one congregation resides in our own home. That congregation starts with our spouses and extends to our children. And laypersons involved in ministry need to understand that they are likewise vulnerable.

Some lay ministers are singles. Thus, it would appear that they do not have the family commitments that the rest of us do. That is only true in part. Surely some singles are sufficiently free from family responsibilities that they can give more time to their ministries. However, those of us who are married often forget that singles, though they may not have spouses and children, have their own family-type relationships. These relationships function as if they were family. These people comprise their family. Singles need to be reminded of the importance of nurturing these relationships, for they are important to the singles' own well-being. When I encourage singles to become involved in ministry, I always ask them questions about the time they're spending in developing relationships with those who function as their family.

Priority number two is occupation or, more specifically, vocation. The definition of vocation is simply the act of serving God in one's occupation. One's occupation is not merely the earning of money for food on the table and a roof over one's head but is rather an opportunity to praise God. If that's the case, it ranks high in our priorities. Laypersons should never be made to feel that their churchly ministry conflicts with their vocational calling.

Another priority is restoration or recreation. All of us need time for recreation. This takes many different forms. For some it may be a hobby or an athletic event. For others it may be reading. For some it is an afternoon nap. Whatever the case, we all require, physically and emotionally, a time for personal restoration. Spiritually healthy people are those who understand the importance of our physical and emotional well-being.

Another priority is our involvement in churchly ministry. As a pastor I have discovered that it is indeed a joy to train a person for some ministry when that person's family life is in order, vocational calling is clear, and he or she is observing the guidelines for physical and emotional health. I have also discovered that most laypersons respond more positively to invitations to ministry when they know that I, as a clergyman, am first concerned about other aspects of their lives. It would be easy for them to assume that I'm coming to recruit them, attempting to get them to do some work in the church with no concern for other commitments in their lives. If, instead, I come to them recognizing that the ministry in the church is not the only important thing in their lives, then I discover openness. They know they can trust me, for I will never push them into a ministry that conflicts with higher priorities.

It is important for us as pastors to understand why certain people say no to us when we ask them to be involved in a ministry. Admittedly some people say no for poor reasons. But some say no because they have been burned by past experiences. Many laypersons today refuse to be involved in ministry for understandable reasons. Some were mismatched, placed in a ministry that required gifts they did not have. They quit in frustration. How fulfilled they might have been had they been placed in a ministry that called for their gifts. But the major reason laypersons refuse to be involved in ministry is because in the past they failed to say no to the wrong ministries after they said yes to the right ministry. As a result, they quickly become overloaded. After great frustration, often resulting in the neglect of their families, they joined the ranks of the burned-out laypersons. This frustration could have been prevented had they learned to maintain the proper priorities in their lives.

III. Preventing Burnout

How can we prevent burnout? It seems to me that we can follow certain steps as pastors to prevent laypersons from being burned out in ministry. What things can we as pastors do?

(1) Include a sabbatical in the lay ministry schedule. A sabbatical is a seventh year in which one is relieved from work. I'm not suggesting that lay ministries should have every seventh year off! That might be too much to bear. I am suggesting that we plan schedules that include restoration and recreation. Allow laypersons to know that they have the same opportunities for vacation from ministry that we as pastors have from ours.

Several years ago while training lay pastors, we had what we called the 22/2 Plan. That meant 22 months on the job, 2 months off. I discovered that 22 months was too long without a break. We switched to an 11/1 Plan. Yes, you guessed it, 11 months on, and then 1 month off. Admittedly, 22/2 has a nicer sound to it than 11/1, but we discovered that lay pastors need a break from their ministry more than once every two years.

(2) Plan periodic evaluation times with each layperson to examine the fruitfulness of his or her ministry. Find out how he or she is feeling about that ministry. Much of the restlessness that suddenly explodes in lay ministry activities could be prevented if we as pastors would meet more regularly with those in ministry positions to know how they are feeling. Some ministries need to have cutoff dates or termination points. Some of our laity would volunteer more quickly for a particular ministry if they knew that in doing so they would not be locked into that position for the rest of their living days! One lady said to me, "I'm scared to volunteer for that job. I would love to do it; I just don't want to do it for the next century. Experience has taught me that if you volunteer for something, you can never get away from it." Many lay ministry positions lend themselves well to having termination dates.

(3) Emphasize the importance of ministry to one's family. (4) Stress the vocational ministry. Let your laity know how important their occupational commitments really are. One of the ways that we as pastors can demonstrate this is to occasionally show up on the job—their job, in this case. This obviously cannot always be done, but many laypersons are excited to show us around the place where they work. (5) Emphasize the importance of personal restoration and recreation. (6) Stress the importance of building one's ministry upon one's gifts. This reduces stress greatly. (7) Teach laypersons how and when to say no. Some of your laypersons will be shocked when you tell them that you're going to teach them how to say no to you. They'll be excited to learn that you're interested in protecting them from overloads.

(8) Underscore the fact that the need does not constitute the call. This is closely related to the statement above. Every open door to ministry is not a summons to the layperson. (9) Help laypersons understand the difference between genuine convic-

tion (which may come from not being involved in an appropriate ministry) and false guilt (which can cause a person to overcommit himself or herself). (10) Help laypersons to pace themselves in their ministries. Teach them to think long-range. Some laypersons attack their ministries as if the world were to be saved by last night. That is a good way for laypersons to drain themselves physically, emotionally, and spiritually. (11) Affirm the fact that all ministry is big business. No ministry is unimportant to God. Pastors, we need to help our laypersons understand that the things they are doing are truly big business—not only in the sight of God but also in the sight of their pastor.

IV. COMMISSIONING LAYPERSONS FOR MINISTRY

Being sent for ministry does not mean I'm going around the world. It may mean I'm merely going next door. Regardless of our ministry—whether it is preaching to thousands or sweeping the basement Sunday School rooms—it is exciting to know that we are sent by the church. Being sent means we are, with the support of the Christian community, placed in a position where we can continue the ministry of Christ. This includes our vocation as well as our churchly ministries. It is appropriate that the church acknowledge persons moving into ministry opportunities through a commissioning service. This is not always possible. Sometimes it is more proper for a few fellow believers to gather for prayer for a layperson as he or she moves into a particular lay ministry opportunity.

There are many creative ways that Christians can celebrate the sending of one of their members into ministry. We are going to look at two such services right now. The first one is a lay ministry covenant. Covenants are an important part of the Christian faith. A covenant is a promise or a commitment; it is something to which we pledge ourselves. A covenant is not to be entered into lightly; however, it is to be entered into with expressions of joy and anticipation. The following covenant is written for use in a formal, public worship setting, yet it may also be used with a small group. The goal of this covenant is to assist believers in pledging before God and each other to function as God's ministers in the world.

Many of us, however, come from theological backgrounds that seldom used covenants in public worship. Thus, using a public liturgy may be too distracting to some. A covenant service should certainly not be forced on those who are unable to appreciate its content. Yet at the same time, there is much value in the stating of truths together as a body. That is what a covenant is. It is an affirmation of certain things that we hold true. It is my prayer that the covenant will be used as a time for self-examination. May it be used with reverence.

I realize that many of you are reading this book in the privacy of your home. You are not in a public worship setting where the covenant can be used in its normal manner. It can still, however, be useful to you as a time for personal spiritual renewal and commitment.

Lay Ministry Covenant

L = Leader; C = Congregation

L: Father, we are Your people.

C: We are the *laos,* the people of God.

L: We are living stones.

C: We are holy priests.

L: We, along with all Christians, are the chosen race, the King's priests.

C: Yes, Father, we are Your priests.

L: We, along with Christians around the world, form a holy nation.

C: Father, we are Your holy nation, we are Your people.

L: Though we are unworthy, we are priests.

C: How humbled we are to be called Your priests, Father.

L: We offer the sacrifices of praise and service and deeds of love.

C: We offer ourselves as sacrifices, desiring that our lives would be spent in ministry.

L: We are the Body of Christ.

LEFT SIDE: Yes, we are part of Your Church.

RIGHT SIDE: And You are the Head.

L: The Incarnation continues.

LEFT SIDE: Yes, it continues in us.

RIGHT SIDE: Thus, we touch lives.

L: We know it is not us, Father.

C: But really You touching through us.

LEFT SIDE: We are honored, Father.

RIGHT SIDE: Yes, honored, but humbled.

L: We thank You for our vocations.

C: And for the ministry we enjoy therein.

L: We thank You for our Christian fellowship.

C: And for the ministry we enjoy therein.

L: We are part of a rich heritage.

C: Of a long lineage of ministers—

L: Persons who understood they were the people of God.

C: And persons who understood the call to service. Scripture (Eph. 4:11): "It was he who gave some to be apostles, some to be prophets, some to be evangelists, and some to be pastors and teachers."

L: We thank You, Father, for equippers.

C: Yes, Father, for they will teach us to minister.

L: We thank You for our equippers.

C: For we rely upon them for our ministry.

L: Yes, Father, we are Your ministers.

LEFT SIDE: And we are all ministers

RIGHT SIDE: And we are as well.

L: And we all are gifted by God.

C: Yes, He has given us gifts for our ministry.

L: We want to minister.

C: Yes, Father, we covenant together and with You that we will use our gifts to minister.

L: We see gifts in each other.

LEFT SIDE: We affirm your gifts.

RIGHT SIDE: And we affirm yours.

L: We recognize the importance of love.

C: Yes, Father, and we desire our ministries to be characterized by it.

L: Our gifts are important.

C: Yet nothing is as important as love.

L: We are embarking on an important mission.

C: And for that mission we are being trained.

L: It's an important mission.

C: And on that mission we are being sent.

L: Father, You have given us each other.

C: We really do need each other.

L: We minister as the Body of Christ.

C: We really do need each other.

L: Yes, we do.

LEFT SIDE: We need you for our ministries.

RIGHT SIDE: And we need you for our ministries.

SING TOGETHER: "The Bond of Love"

> *We are one in the bond of love;*
> *We are one in the bond of love.*
> *We have joined our spirit with the Spirit of God;*
> *We are one in the bond of love.**

L: We are ready to begin.

LEFT SIDE: Yes.

L: We know we are called to minister.

RIGHT SIDE: Yes.

L: We are gifted for ministry.

LEFT SIDE: Yes, we are.

L: We have equippers to train us for ministry.

RIGHT SIDE: Yes, we do.

L: We have the church to send us for ministry.

C: Yes, and we need those who send us, for they encourage and strengthen us in our ministry.

L: Therefore,

L AND C: We covenant this day to begin to fulfill our ministry.

LEFT SIDE: Serving as You served.

RIGHT SIDE: Giving as You gave.

LEFT SIDE: Touching as You touched.

RIGHT SIDE: Hurting as You hurt.

LEFT SIDE: Through our ministry we will experience joy.

RIGHT SIDE: Yes, and through our ministry we may experience death.

L: We confess our need of You.

C: And our complete dependence upon You.

L AND C: And our thankfulness for the opportunity to serve.

(A time of silent prayer or Communion may follow.)

The purpose of the commissioning service is exactly as the term would imply—to commission or delegate laypersons to specific ministries. The commissioning service can be one of the most exciting events in your church. It can be a meaningful service! It is a time when laypersons examine their hearts before they give themselves to ministry. At the same time the congregation pledges their support, their love, and their prayers on behalf of these laypersons going into ministry. It is a sobering and joyful time. The following is a lay ministry commissioning service. You may want to adapt and change it to fit your particular situation. As the writer of this commissioning service, I encourage you to use it as it will best serve the needs of the persons being commissioned.

Lay Ministry Commissioning Service
Pastor states the following:

The ministry that you are about to begin will bring you much joy and fulfillment. At the same time it may bring into your pathway great challenges. Sometimes ministry brings heartaches. It is for this reason that you have entered into this moment thoughtfully, carefully, and prayerfully. You will be giving of all that God has given you. All that you possess you give to Him. In a very real sense you offer yourself to God as a sacrifice.

Having committed yourself to ministry in the privacy of your heart, you now make that commitment in the presence of these, your brothers and sisters. By their presence, they are saying they accept the responsibility of encouraging you in your ministry. They pledge themselves to you as you commit yourself to service.

Questioning of the Candidate for Lay Ministry:
1. Do you believe you have been called to ministry? (Answer "Yes, I do.")
2. Do you recognize the gifts God has given you and the ways in which they can be used for His service? (Answer "Yes, I do.")
3. Have you availed yourself on instruction and training that can enhance your service? (Answer "Yes, I have.")
4. Are you now ready to be sent forth into your ministry by this fellowship of believers? (Answer "Yes, I am.")

5. Do you desire your life to be lived in service to God and to your fellow human beings? (Answer "Yes, I do.")

Questioning of the Fellowship:
Do you pledge to support those who begin new ministries? Will you pray for them? Will you encourage them both in deeds and in words? If so, answer, "We will." (Answer "We will.")

Prayer of Consecration: (candidates kneeling)
Father, every day with You has meaning, but this day is especially meaningful. We come to You, committing ourselves to Your service. We are conscious of the example of the ministry of Your Son Jesus. May ours be a continuation of the work He started. Accept our activities today as a sign of our love for You and of thankfulness for what You have done.

We commit these ministers—these Your people—to You. May their ministries be fruitful. In Jesus' name. Amen.

To the Candidates:
It is a joyful task for me indeed, before God and your brothers and sisters in Christ, to commission you to the ministry to which you have been called.* The God who has called you will also sustain you. Amen.

*Note—Rather than the words "to which you have been called," you may want to insert the specific ministry. For example, you may say "to the ministry of Sunday School teaching" or "to the ministry of home visitation." If this service is used in conjunction with vocational callings, then it would be appropriate to say "to the ministry of dentistry" or "to the ministry of carpentry."

Laypersons, congratulations on beginning your ministry. For many of you I probably ought to say congratulations on continuing your ministry. Most of you who have read the previous pages have been involved in many ministries through the years. It is laypeople like you who make pastors like us so excited about our calling. It is a thrill to function as your equippers!

Appendix A
From Discovering My Gift to Finding My Ministry

Having discovered your gift(s), let's look at some options of ministry. The following list comes from Tim Blanchard's book *A Practical Guide to Finding Your Spiritual Gifts*. The headings are the 13 gifts listed by Blanchard. Below each gift are some of his suggested ministries.

A. *Preaching*
   1. boards and commissions
   2. Bible teacher
      migrant worker, prisons, hospitals, rest homes, military
   3. pastor
   4. missionary
      church planting, evangelism
   5. gospel teams
      evangelistic services, speaker

B. *Teaching*
   1. boards and commissions
      elder, deacon, Christian education
   2. church services
      toddler church, beginner church, primary church
   3. home visitation
   4. young people
      Boy Scouts, Girl Scouts
   5. outreach
      gospel team, small-group home Bible study leader
   6. Sunday School
      superintendent, assistant superintendent, department coordinator, children's teacher, youth teacher, adult teacher, substitute teacher
   7. Vacation Bible School
      committee, teacher, assistant
   8. missionary-teacher
   9. international student
      ministry, teacher

C. *Knowledge*
1. boards and commissions
   elder, deacon, Christian education
2. young people
   Boy Scouts, Girl Scouts
3. outreach
   small-group home Bible study discussion leader
4. Sunday School
   superintendent, assistant superintendent, youth teacher, adult teacher
5. Vacation Bible School
   teacher
6. missionary
   translation, interpretation—commentaries
7. research
   Sunday School curriculum, Bible school curriculum

D. *Wisdom*
1. boards and commissions
   elder, deacon, trustee, school commission, building commission
2. librarian
3. outreach
   home visitation, small-group home Bible study leader, gospel teams
4. young people
   youth sponsors, Boy Scouts, Girl Scouts, teen week speaker
5. counseling
   vocational, minority group programs, gang ministries, marriage, homosexuals, divorced, released prisoners, widows and widowers
6. missionary
   planning, church planting, school instruction
7. Vacation Bible School
   director

E. *Exhortation*
1. boards and commissions
   elder, deacon, Christian education
2. church services
   toddler, beginner, primary, adult, vocal music, usher, greeter
3. visitation
   sick, newcomers, shut-ins, canvassing, members, prison, hospital, rest homes, telephone
4. young people
   Boy Scouts, Girl Scouts

5. outreach
gospel teams
6. counselor
emotionally disturbed, divorced, premarital, gangs, homosexuals, juvenile offenders, marital conflicts, narcotic addicts, potential suicides, released prison offenders, runaway youths, school dropouts, widows and widowers, camp
7. Vacation Bible School
teacher

F. *Faith*
1. boards and commissions
elder, deacon, trustee, nominating committee, missionary commission
2. outreach
home visitation, gospel teams, evangelism
3. missionary
church planting

G. *Discernment of Spirits*
1. boards and commissions
elder, deacon, membership commission, Christian education commission, nominating committee, missionary commission, school commission
2. personnel recruitment
3. outreach
home visitation
4. young people
youth sponsors
5. counselors
church, camp, juvenile offenders, marital conflicts, divorced, neglected children, neglectful parents, runaway youth, potential suicide, school dropouts
6. librarian
7. Sunday School
adult

H. *Helps*
1. boards and commissions
deaconess, social commission, trustee, finance commission, property commission, school commission, building commission
2. officers
treasurer, financial secretary, clerk
3. church services
usher, greeter

4. librarian
5. nursery
   coordinator, assistant
6. missionary
   local missionary society leader
7. men's or women's fellowship
   committee
8. outreach
   gospel teams—transportation, Bible school host, home Bible
   study host
9. Sunday School
   secretary, departmental secretary
10. music
    chancel choir director, youth choir director, children's choir
    director, song leader, choir member, soloist, duet, trio, quartet,
    pianist (accompanist, soloist), organist, instrumentalist, orchestra
    leader, music committee
11. bus driver
12. banquet worker
13. office help
    type, draw, file, assemble, reproduce materials, mailings,
    telephoning, record information, key punching
14. hospitality
    meals, lodging
15. transportation
    shut-ins, youth activities, church services
16. cook
17. nurse
18. kitchen help
19. athletic teams
    basketball, baseball/softball, volleyball, swimming, football,
    other _____
20. maintenance
    landscaping, carpentry, painting, electrical, plumbing, cleaning
21. artistic work
22. financial
    accounting, bookkeeping, money counting, computer
23. audiovisual
    videotaping, projectionist, filing, printer/posters, television,
    photographer, artist, tape recorder
24. Sunday School
    hear memory work, secretary
25. helper
    deaf, blind, narcotic addicts, alcoholics, mentally ill, migrant
    workers, remedial reading, nursing, underprivileged, mentally
    retarded
26. library bookbinding

27. radio booth
    sound engineer
28. drama—acting

I. *Serving*
   1. officers
      financial secretary, treasurer
   2. librarian
   3. greeter
   4. building committee
   5. nursery coordinator
   6. young people
      Boy Scouts, Girl Scouts
   7. local missionary society
   8. men's or women's fellowship
   9. music
      song leader, soloist, instrumentalist
   10. nurse
   11. kitchen help
   12. handyperson
   13. carpenter
   14. church drama productions
   15. financial
   16. accounting
   17. audiovisual
       videotaping, projectionist, television, photographer
   18. helper
       narcotic addicts, alcoholics, migrant workers, nursing,
       underprivileged
   19. music
       chancel choir director, youth choir director, children's choir
       director, song leader, choir member, soloist, duet, trio, quartet,
       pianist (accompanist, soloist), organist, instrumentalist, orchestra
       leader, music committee
   20. office help
       type, telephone
   21. hospitality
       meals, lodging

J. *Administration*
   1. boards and commissions
      deacon, trustee, deaconess, Christian education, missionary,
      school, property, finance, membership, evangelistic, church
      services, social, building, planning
   2. officers
      financial secretary, treasurer, head usher

3. nursery coordinator
4. young people
   youth sponsor, youth committee, single adults' sponsor
5. local missionary society leader
6. men's or women's fellowship leader
7. Sunday School
   assistant superintendent, department coordinator—all ages, class officer, class committees
8. librarian cataloging
9. international student ministry
10. camp
    director, assistant director, administrative staff
11. radio booth operator
12. audiovisual room coordinator
13. drama directing
14. coffeehouse ministry
15. Vacation Bible School
    director, committee, assistant
16. teen week director

K. *Ruling*
   1. boards and commissions
      school board, deacon, trustee, property, finance, building, planning
   2. church services
      greeter, head usher
   3. church moderator
      vice moderator
   4. Vacation Bible School director
   5. teen week director
   6. Sunday School
      superintendent, department coordinator
   7. men's fellowship leader
   8. women's fellowship leader
   9. local missionary society leader
   10. camp director
   11. class officers

L. *Mercy*
   1. boards and commissions
      deacon, deaconess
   2. church services
      usher, greeter
   3. cassette ministry to shut-ins
   4. hospitality
      meals, lodging

5. visitation

    sick, dying, shut-ins, hospitals, rest homes, telephone, newcomers, bereaved

6. missions

    committee, missionary circles, local gospel mission, correspondent with missionaries, furlough assistant

7. helper

    alcoholics, mentally ill, remedial reading, nursing, blind, deaf, gangs, hungry and underprivileged, mentally retarded, migrant workers, narcotic addict, released prison offenders

---

M. *Giving*

    1. boards and commissions

        trustee, missionary commission, fund-raising commission, building commission, school commission, planning and development commission

    2. food and money to help poor

    3. hospitality

        meals, lodging

    4. sponsor and underwrite special missionary projects

Appendix B
Definitions of Gifts

PROPHECY:

> The gift of prophecy is the ability to comprehend a message from God and transmit it to a particular audience with clarity and authority, through a communication channel such as preaching or writing.

HELPING:

> The gift of helps is the ability to be of assistance to some other person in the performance of their particular assignment in the church.

TEACHING:

> The gift of teaching is the capacity to present information or concepts in such a way that people can remember the information and understand the concepts; in other words, they learn.

ENCOURAGING:

> The gift of encouraging is the ability to minister to others by word and deed in such a way that they receive comfort, counsel, and courage for their tasks.

GIVING:

> The gift of giving includes both the ability to earn material resources and the willingness to let these resources be used for maximum benefit to the kingdom of God.

LEADERSHIP:

> Leadership is the ability to "be out in front" of a group, setting goals in accord with God's will and enlisting the harmonious efforts of the group to achieve these goals.

MERCY:

> The gift of mercy is the ability to sense the feelings of those who hurt, whether they are Christian or non-Christian, and, in a cheerful and effective manner, to help them cope with their problems.

PASTOR:

The gift of pastor is the capacity to oversee and care for the spiritual wholeness of a group of believers.

APOSTLE:

The gift of apostle is the ability to assume and exercise leadership over churches with a special effectiveness in increasing the number of churches or in introducing the church into new areas or to new cultures.

MISSIONARY:

The gift of missionary is the ability to minister effectively in a second culture.

EVANGELIST:

The gift of evangelist is the ability to share the gospel with unbelievers in such a way that they accept Christ and become believers. It includes a spiritual sensitivity to discern the readiness of persons to respond and may be exercised by both laypersons and clergy in individual or group encounters.

WORD OF WISDOM:

The word of wisdom is a spiritual gift that involves the ability to take knowledge and make appropriate applications to problem situations. It is the ability to make proper choices in difficult situations based on sufficient information.

WORD OF KNOWLEDGE:

The gift of knowledge is the ability to discover, analyze, and remember information important to the growth and well-being of the Body.

DISCERNMENT OF SPIRITS:

The gift of discernment is the gift of being able to distinguish between the working of the human spirit and the divine Spirit or between the works of God and the works of Satan; the ability to recognize false teaching or to perceive divine truth in confusing situations; a God-guided instinct to know right from wrong.

HEALING:

The gift of healing is the capacity whereby some individuals are uniquely used of God at certain times to be the intermediary through whom God's healing power is applied to another person's physical or emotional need.

MIRACLES:

The gift of miracles is the ability to exercise faith in such a way that others perceive that what has happened can have no other explanation than the intervention of God into the natural order of events.

FAITH:

Faith as a gift of the Holy Spirit refers to an extraordinary ability to discern the will and purpose of God for the future of His work and to act accordingly.

SERVING:

The gift of serving is the capacity to identify and perform countless small tasks that need to be done for the efficient operation of the Body of Christ. While the gift of helps is centered on assisting another person to do their assigned task, the gift of service is centered on doing those small necessary tasks that may otherwise go undone and usually relates to the institution or a group.

LANGUAGES:

The gift of languages is that of an increased ability to learn and comprehend a second language for the purpose of communicating the gospel.

INTERPRETATION OF LANGUAGES:

The gift of interpretation of languages is a heightening of the ability to understand the gospel in one language and express it without distortion in another language.

Taken from: *Strategy Manual for Finding Your Ministry,* by Raymond Hurn.

Reference Notes

PREFACE

1. Howard Butt, *At the Edge of Hope* (New York: Seabury Press, 1978), 78-79.

2. Carlyle Marney, *Priests to Each Other* (Valley Forge, Pa.: Judson Press, 1974), 9.

3. Elton Trueblood, *Your Other Vocation* (New York: Harper and Brothers, 1952), 29.

4. Thomas Gillespie, "The Laity in Biblical Perspective," *The New Laity*, ed. Ralph D. Bucy (Waco, Tex.: Word Books, 1978), 32.

CHAPTER 1

1. Kenneth Chafin, *Help! I'm a Layman* (Waco, Tex.: Word Books, 1966), 1.

2. Oscar Feucht, *Everyone a Minister* (St. Louis: Concordia Publishing House, 1974), 37.

3. Gillespie, "The Laity in Biblical Perspective," 17.

4. Ibid., 20.

5. Hans Küng, *The Church* (Garden City, N.Y.: Image Books, 1967), 478.

6. Feucht, *Everyone a Minister*, 40.

7. Butt, *At the Edge of Hope*, 79.

8. Francis O. Ayers, *The Ministry of the Laity* (Philadelphia: Westminster Press, 1962), 25.

CHAPTER 2

1. Hendrik Kraemer, *A Theology of the Laity* (Philadelphia: Westminster Press, 1958), 137.

2. Ibid., 48-49.

3. Richard Harrington, "The Ministry of All Christians" (Ph.D. diss., Drew University, 1979), 19.

4. William Barclay, *Acts* (Philadelphia: Westminster Press, 1953), 1.

5. Ibid., 2.

6. Ibid.

7. Donald McGavran, *Understanding Church Growth* (Grand Rapids: Wm. B. Eerdmans Publishing Co., 1970), 16.

8. Clifford Wright, *Laymen Are Ministers* (Melbourne, Australia: Methodist Federal Board of Education, Methodist Church of Australia, 1961), 12-13.

9. *Book of Discipline* of the United Methodist Church (Nashville: United Methodist Publishing House, 1968), 106.

10. Hans-Ruedi Weber, "Ministries of the Priestly People," *Laity*, No. 9 (July, 1960): 19-20.

11. Howard Grimes, "The Vocation of the Laity," *Perkins School of Theology Journal* 13, No. 1 (Fall, 1959): 1.

12. Albert C. Outler, "The Pastoral Office," *Perkins School of Theology Journal* 16, No. 1 (Fall, 1962): 5.

13. Trueblood, *Your Other Vocation*, 58.

14. Ibid., 62.

15. Alden Kelley, *The People of God* (Greenwich, Conn.: Seabury Press, 1962), 56.

16. Trueblood, *Your Other Vocation*, 63.

17. Ibid., 66.

18. Gillespie, "The Laity in Biblical Perspective," 24.

19. Second Assembly of the World Council of Churches, 1954.

CHAPTER 3

1. Trueblood, *Your Other Vocation*, 43.

2. Küng, *The Church*, 492.

3. Ibid., 493.

4. Christopher Brooke, *The Layman in Christian History*, eds. Stephen Charles Neill and Hans-Ruedi Weber (Philadelphia: Westminster Press, 1963), 111.

5. Ignatius, cited in *History of the Christian Church*, by Philip Schaff (Philadelphia: John C. Winston Co., 1933), 59.

6. Küng, *The Church*, 483.

7. Van A. Harvey, *A Handbook of Theological Terms* (New York: Macmillan Co., 1969), 250.

8. Gordon Rupp, "The Age of the Reformation," *The Layman in Christian History*, 142, citing William Tyndale, "Wicked Mammon," *Doctrinal Treatises* (Parker Soc. ed.), 101-3.

9. Franz Hildebrandt, *Christianity According to the Wesleys* (London: Epworth Press, 1956), 48.

10. Stephen Charles Neill, "Britain," *The Layman in Christian History*, 207.

11. For a more extensive discussion of Wesley's use of the laity, see James L. Garlow, "John Wesley's Understanding of the Laity as Demonstrated by His Use of the Lay Preachers" (Ph.D. diss., Drew University, 1979).

CHAPTER 4

1. James F. Engel and H. Wilbert Norton, *What's Gone Wrong with the Harvest?* (Grand Rapids: Zondervan Publishing Co., 1975), 140.

2. For a fuller discussion of the characteristics of agape, see Anders Nygren, *Agape and Eros* (Philadelphia: Westminster Press, 1932).

3. A. T. Robertson and Alfred Plummer, *I Corinthians* (Edinburgh: T. and T. Clark, 1911), 285.

4. Ray Stedman, *Body Life* (Gendale, Calif.: Regal Books, 1972), 51-52.

5. Leslie B. Flynn, *Nineteen Gifts of the Spirit* (Wheaton, Ill.: Victor Books, 1974), 22.

6. Raymond W. Hurn, *Finding Your Ministry* (Kansas City: Beacon Hill Press of Kansas City, 1979), 21.

7. Stedman, *Body Life*, 40-41.

8. Kenneth Kinghorn, *Gifts of the Spirit* (Nashville: Abingdon Press, 1976), 37.

9. David L. Hocking, *The World's Greatest Church* (Long Beach, Calif.: Sounds of Grace Ministries, 1976), 134-37.

CHAPTER 5

1. A. W. Kist, "Dynamics of Adult Education," *Laity*, No. 23 (July, 1967): 23.

2. Edwin Carl Linberg, "An Examination of the Role of the Clergy as Enabler of the Development and Growth of the Ministry of the Laity" (D.Min. diss., School of Theology at Claremont, Calif., 1975), 246-47.

3. Ibid.

4. These five words—*association, impartation, demonstration, delegation,* and *supervision*—are borrowed from the chapter titles of Robert Coleman's book *The Master Plan of Evangelism* (Old Tappan, N.J.: Fleming H. Revell Co., 1963).

5. Linberg, "The Clergy as Enabler of the Laity," 244-45.

6. Arnold B. Come, "Lay Training in the U.S.A.," *Laity,* No. 19 (July, 1965): 15.

7. Tim Blanchard, *A Practical Guide to Finding Your Spiritual Gifts* (Wheaton, Ill.: Tyndale House Publishers, 1979).

8. Frederick Norwood, "The Shaping of Methodist Ministry," *Religion in Life* 45, No. 3 (Autumn, 1974): 350.

9. David Mains, *Full Circle* (Waco, Tex.: Word Books, 1971).

10. W. H. Fitchett, *Wesley and His Century* (New York: Eaton and Mains, 1906), 219-20.

CHAPTER 6

1. Charles Lake, "To Go or Not to Go?" *OMS Outreach,* No. 2 (1978): 13.

2. Kraemer, *A Theology of the Laity,* 127.

3. Hans-Ruedi Weber, *Salty Christians* (New York: Seabury Press, 1963), 49.

4. For an excellent discussion of the advantages of "Amateur Status," see Trueblood, *Your Other Vocation,* 39-42.